Praise for *Story Work*

"GG Renee Hill's vulnerability is both courageous and contagious. She shows us how we can all cast off the burden of shame by spilling our secrets onto the page, wrapping our wounds in words, and finding healing in the power of storytelling."

—**Javacia Harris Bowser**, founder of See Jane Write and author of *Find Your Way Back: How to Write Your Way Through Anything*

"In *Story Work*, GG Renee Hill does more than teach the art of storytelling; she embodies it. With raw honesty and heartfelt reflection, she models the very method of *story work* she invites you to explore. With intimate personal narratives, carefully crafted reflection questions, and guided exercises, this book is not just something you read—it's something you experience. Bringing intention and care, GG Renee Hill gently moves alongside you, helping you uncover, shape, and honor your stories. I paused in each chapter to breathe in its beauty, depth, and invitation to step more fully into my story. Whether you are a writer, an artist, an activist, or someone longing to understand yourself more deeply, this book is a gift. Those who journey through its pages will not only witness the power of storytelling—they will emerge transformed by it."

—**Cierra Kaler-Jones**, storyteller, teaching artist, cultural organizer, and director of Unlock Your Story

"*Story Work* is a beautiful guide for turning pain into power; into story. GG Renee Hill empowers us into self-discovery, reminding us that we can use our barriers as fuel for transformation. With poignant stories of life with her mother as an

engine, Hill illuminates the room: We *can* reclaim our voices and shape our own paths."

—**Chelene Knight**, author of *Let It Go: Free Yourself from Old Beliefs and Find a New Path to Joy*, and *Safekeeping: A Writer's Guided Journal for Launching a Book with Love*

"Let me say this: I thought I understood the power of storytelling before reading *Story Work*, but this takes it to a whole different level. GG Renee Hill doesn't just tell a story—she invites you in, pulls up a chair, and makes you feel like you're right there with her. Every chapter feels like a look into Hill's heart—intimate, vivid, and so vulnerable. The way she shares her relationship with her mother and navigates the complexities of mental illness? Whew. It transcended the pages. I saw my own family, my own memories reflected back at me. I know there are so many of you who will see yourselves in these stories too.

"Hill is a remarkable storyteller—the kind who makes you smell the Blue Magic hair grease, hear the soundtrack of the '90s, and feel the weight of every moment. What stayed with me most was her invitation to lean into curiosity—one of my top character strengths—and her gentle observations that don't force, just allow you to be. With each prompt, I could feel myself peeling back the layers of my own story, and it felt really good to my soul. There are books about self-help and development . . . and then there's this one. Those books are like chicken broth. Warm, and they'll hold you over. This book is like a hot bowl of good Southern chili with a side of Grandma's cornbread! You will leave filled with healing, and it's going to stick to your bones."

—**Chianti Lomax**, executive coach and author of *Evolving While Black: The Ultimate Guide to Happiness and Transformation on Your Own Terms*

"*Story Work* is a book anyone who has ever felt like an outlier can count on to feel seen and understood. Hill's poignant perspective around the possibility that awaits on the other side of telling our stories is a liberating message of second chances and new beginnings. Gentle, thoughtful, and relatable, her stories are honest and vulnerable as Hill crystalizes what it means to reframe your past and your path—without judgment and with deep care."

—**Chloe Dulce Louvouezo**, storyteller, creative strategist, author of *Life, I Swear: Intimate Stories from Black Women on Identity, Healing, and Self-Trust*

"*Story Work* is a soulful, truth-telling companion for anyone ready to examine the stories they've been told—and the ones they've been telling themselves. With tenderness and clarity, GG Renee Hill invites us to witness her journey of rewriting a painful past and reclaiming her power through the page. Her words are both balm and blueprint, reminding us that healing is not about having the perfect story but about having the courage to keep writing new chapters. This is the kind of book you return to again and again—dog-eared, highlighted, and held close."

—**L'Oreal Thompson Payton**, award-winning journalist and author of *Stop Waiting for Perfect: Step Out of Your Comfort Zone and Into Your Power*

"In this heartfelt and deeply personal book, GG Renee Hill offers invaluable strategies for transforming pain into power. A must-read for anyone seeking to reclaim their strength and heal the wounds of past trauma."

—**Monique Rainford-Bourne**, MD, MBA, author of *Pregnant While Black: Advancing Justice for Maternal Health in America*

"With her vivid and vulnerable writing, GG Renee Hill gently guides us to our own inner sage. By sharing her own story of how writing led her back to herself, Hill offers generous and insight-inspiring journal prompts that give us permission to do the same. A treasure of a book."

—**Karen Walrond**, author of *The Lightmaker's Manifesto*, *Radiant Rebellion*, and *In Defense of Dabbling*

STORY WORK

STORY WORK

Field Notes on Self-Discovery and Reclaiming Your Narrative

GG RENEE HILL

Broadleaf Books
Minneapolis

STORY WORK
Field Notes on Self-Discovery and Reclaiming Your Narrative

30 29 28 27 26 25 1 2 3 4 5 6 7 8 9

Library of Congress Control Number: 2025930372 (print)

This is a work of nonfiction based on the author's memories and reflections. The names of some individuals have been changed to respect their privacy.

Cover image: © 2025 Getty Images; Abstract Street Map inspired Background Illustration/1334341993 by Charles Harker
Cover design by Faceout Studio, Addie Lutzo

Print ISBN: 979-8-8898-3265-2
eBook ISBN: 979-8-8898-3266-9

Dedicated to my heartbeats

Contents

Preface

I didn't expect to become a writer. Overwhelmed and disillusioned with life, I went to see a therapist for the first time when I was about twenty-eight years old, and she gave me a writing assignment to answer questions about my childhood. She told me that my story could be a source of strength instead of shame if I changed the way I thought about it. She encouraged me to write about the things I struggled to say out loud. I was intrigued by the thought of finding strength in my story, but I didn't know where to start or if that was even possible.

Writing has always been a safe space for me, but it was a hobby, not a deliberate tool for reflection. The diaries of my childhood were full of imaginary worlds, doodles, and ramblings about cute boys and mean girls. I made lists of my daily outfits, hairstyles I wanted to try, and my favorite TV shows. I wrote stories that were for my eyes only, mostly about the adventures of an imaginary family, where I played out my ideal life through the characters. My diaries encapsulated the innocence of my girlhood. Other than the occasional heartbreak in my teens, I didn't start writing from my soul until I was out of my parents' house with kids of my own, trying to make my way in the world while coping with years of suppressed pain and confusion.

When the therapist said to write about what I was feeling, it was the permission slip I didn't know I was waiting for. I started writing pages and pages of worries, questions, letters, prayers, and confessions, trying to make sense of the fog, confusion, and shame I'd been silently carrying.

My childhood was traumatic in many ways. It took me a long time to admit that because I had loving parents and a caring family, and I was never physically neglected or abused. My mother, who was my favorite person in the world, heard voices that no one else could hear. She showered me with a mix of devotion and delusion daily, while my father helplessly watched his wife unravel, doing his best to show up for me without triggering my mother's paranoia. By the time she was diagnosed with schizophrenia, I was in college, my parents were divorced, and I was certain it was only a matter of time before I started hearing voices too.

For years, I put on the best show I could, trying to appear polished on the outside, while inside I harbored emotional chaos. Everyone seemed to think I was well-adjusted, and I was desperate to maintain that image. Behind the curtain, I was struggling professionally, romantically, socially, financially, emotionally, spiritually. All of it. Throughout my twenties, I survived by compartmentalizing and pretending. The whole time, I carried the belief that I would always be a day late and a dollar short—that I would always struggle because of the hidden wound that never received enough air to breathe and heal.

In many ways, writing saved me. It saved me from living a false life, blindly stumbling along with my fear and avoidance, settling for the fate that I would always be broken. It gave me the language to break my silence and bring my inner world out of the shadows: stories I'd never told, truths I'd never spoken, questions I'd never asked, possibilities I'd never considered. The more I wrote, the more I liberated myself and the more I had an undeniable calling to share this gift with other people. That calling led to significant shifts in my mindset, lifestyle, and career.

I was raised in Pittsburgh, Pennsylvania, a Midwestern city in an Eastern state, known for steel, sports, and smoggy skies. My mother worked as a secretary at Carnegie-Mellon

University in the '80s when I was very young and then at the University of Pittsburgh Medical School when I was a teenager in the early '90s. To enrich my education, she used every resource available to her as part of the collegiate network in the city. That included special access to university-sponsored early childhood education in my formative years and programs, classes, and internships in my precollege years.

When I was growing up, before my mother's symptoms became intrusive, our calendar was full of choir rehearsals, Bible studies, dance, piano, modeling classes, and theater. She was an avid reader and consumer of the arts. The Carnegie Library in Oakland was a second home. The Benedum Center in the Cultural District downtown was our escapism. My dad built a bookshelf into the wall from the ceiling to the floor in our family room to hold her many literary treasures. Her interests ranged from romance to mystery to religion to psychology. I read her Agatha Christie novels over and over again. The ultimate happiness was lying on the couch in the family room, buried in blankets with a book in my hand, my mom across the room in her reclining chair and her own book, the wood-burning stove crackling between us. As I got older, she began to read only spiritual texts. She would take copious notes and sit me down to share what she was learning, and she'd ask me questions to encourage me to read between the lines and apply what I was reading to life. Even when her language became infused with paranoia and delusions, studying Scripture and sacred writings seemed to calm her. In my teens, I remember not wanting to sit still for these study sessions, but it cultivated in me a vigorous curiosity about God, life, and the interiority of other humans.

I've always been tuned in to the emotional currents around me with a fascination for how people see the world, express themselves, and find meaning in this uncertain existence. Even as a child, I cared about everyone in my orbit feeling seen, heard, and included. Playing outside in my neighborhood, I was the one who made up dances, organized games, and wanted all the kids to feel comfortable about the role they were playing. I took my time making friends, gravitating toward kids who cared about doing well in school but didn't take themselves so seriously that they couldn't have fun too. I loved collecting friends here and there and bringing them together. So if I met someone new in class, chorus, dance, or church who was on the same wavelength, I wanted them to then meet all of my friends so we could bond over our shared vibes. I was quiet and didn't like to be the center of attention, but I was also a natural community builder.

Through college, internships, and jobs, I collected kindred spirits in likely and unlikely packages. Going to a historically Black university, I met people who had the same brown skin as me but came from different backgrounds and cultures across the diaspora. I started getting corporate experience at seventeen years old as an intern at US Steel, where I bonded with people decades older than me, of different races and economic classes, but able to find the shared values and unifying humanity underneath our differences. While my closest friend groups have predominantly been comprised of Black girls, whether it's school, work, or creative community, I welcome and attract diversity in friendship and connection.

In my relationships, I'm a comforter, active listener, cheerleader, and safe space. I long for people to shed pretense and share their more vulnerable layers in my presence. I love to watch people's eyes light up when talking about their interests and passions, their smiles when they talk about their families and loved ones. I was never good at small talk; you could tell me what you got for your birthday, and I would ask what those gifts meant to you. You could tell me that you're Italian, and I would want to talk about your family history and how it shaped your worldview. In hindsight, it makes perfect sense that this instinct led me to the work I do now—writing and teaching about inner reflection and outer expression.

My inquisitive nature forged beautiful connections, but it also planted seeds of doubt because I wasn't confident in who I was. I noticed how little the dominant culture seemed to value these deeper layers. In social settings, people wanted to talk about possessions, credentials, and social status, and I wanted to talk about heart and soul. I got too many funny looks and sideways comments over the years to believe that my propensities could serve any valued, worldly purpose. So I was a quiet observer in loud social gatherings and invested my time and energy into more intimate one-on-one connections. Eventually, I began to seek other outlets for this part of me.

I created a blog in 2009, a few years after I started therapy. It was inspired by the natural hair movement in the Black community, which brought an explosion of voices and creative expression into my life that awakened my inner artist. As I joined the chorus of voices rediscovering and appreciating their natural hair, I was also having a similar rediscovery with my inner authentic self, and I rode the wave of that collective energy. I wrote publicly about my mother's mental illness and my own mental health, self-discovery, and identity. The more I wrote, the more I discovered people who were drawn to the vulnerability and honesty that I once thought was a weakness. Soon I wasn't just writing for myself; I was writing for them too.

There's a life-changing shift that happens when you realize that no matter what you've been through, your story can be a source of strength for you and others. By sharing my words online and finding a creative community, I was reclaiming my story, one truth at a time. The thought of my story helping someone else gave me hope, and I nurtured that hope every time I sat down to write.

At thirty-five, I left my career in financial services and set out to turn my calling into a creative career. Since then, I've self-published books and created blogs, workshops, and coaching programs that emphasize self-care, break down barriers to expression, and explore individual and group narratives. Through my website allthemanylayers.com and my social media platforms, I've built an engaged community of supporters who find healing and purpose in examining their life stories for personal and professional growth and well-being. In 2018, my essay "Choosing My Mental Health over My Mother" was published on Shondaland.com, and I still receive emails and messages from people all over the world who grew up with a mentally ill parent or family member like I did and have struggled to find peace in their lives as adults. They share their stories with me and ask if I have any advice to help them cope. The personal stories and mindset shifts in *Story Work* are my offering to them and to anyone who struggles with a defeated outlook due to their life circumstances and self-concept.

Story Work delivers the transformative message that no matter where you start or what struggles you face, life can be expansive, abundant, and full of creative potential. The difficulties that shaped you don't have to define you. You can look at your life with curiosity instead of judgment and then, over time, with a sense of creativity and possibility. You can change your narrative from "Oh, well, these are the cards I've been dealt" to "What hope can I create with these cards I've been dealt?"

As writing opened my mind to the idea that I could change my story, my hope is that this book will open your mind—whether you consider yourself a writer or not—and empower you to find new pathways for your story too.

Acknowledgments

I am full of gratitude to my partner and kids for riding the waves with me and making sacrifices so that I could make room in our lives for this work. To my mom for instilling her love of God, art, and learning into me. To my dad, whose gentle, sturdy love sustained me through my lost years and still does to this day. To my sister for her unconditional devotion, guidance, and support. To my brothers for making me feel safe and cherished. To my sister-in-love for the encouragement, long talks, and hugs. To my extended family—the Hills and the Hamlins, alive and departed—for the treasured memories, love, prayers, and blessings.

I am also deeply thankful to my chosen family, the soulmates who have seen me through every version of myself. To Vonnie for being my best friend, memory keeper, and mind reader. To Kimmie for being my first creative partner and community. To Trista, Heather, Tamara, Kenya, Kizi, Nikki, Chanell, Tiffany, Netta, Jendayi, Bezi, Felicia, Fawn, Haywood, and Millia for their friendships that have shaped me and persist in different ways through time, change, and distance.

To the families that have welcomed me and treated me as their own—the Cephases, the Jacksons, the Robertsons, the Joneses, and the Woodleys. Thank you for making me feel held when I needed it the most. Thank you for offering grace through my growing pains.

To the bloggers who opened their arms and showed me what a creative community feels like from day one—Jessica,

Jacqueline, Lucy, Shefon, Erica, Ty, Ashley, Yetti, Erica, Roconia, Tassika, and more.

To the Inner Story Writing Circle, Writing the Layers, and Permission to Write communities for the connection, engagement, and inspiration. You have been instrumental in helping me believe in myself, view vulnerability as generosity, embrace the magic in the mess, and choose curiosity over judgment.

To Rachel, Cindy, Stephanie, Erica, Heather, Kimmie, and Tyece for being the early readers of *Story Work* and providing insights that allowed me to step outside of myself and see my story from different angles.

To Ashley Coleman Thomas, Tyece Wilkins-Amadi, Nikki Walton, Delanea Davis, Christina Fonthes, Heather Hopson, Charlottis Woodley, Rachel Nusbaum, and Robin Puett for the collaborations and opportunities that have helped me grow as a writer and facilitator.

To Deesha Dyer, Christine Platt, and Chloe Dulce Louvouezo for generously sharing the knowledge and resources to illuminate this mysterious writing and publishing adventure.

To The Writer's Center for giving me a platform and the opportunities to develop and refine my craft.

To Ashley Hong at Gardner Literary for your warm reception of my idea and for guiding me through the pitching and publication process with the care and attentiveness I needed. To Jarrod Harrison at Broadleaf Books for championing my vision and giving me creative leeway while offering expansive questions and insights that made this book not only deeply personal but also thoroughly universal. To everyone at Gardner Literary and Broadleaf, thank you for making my publishing dream a reality.

To the readers who have been with me since *The Write Curl Diary*, I see you and appreciate you for following me from one project to the next. To the readers who have joined along the way, and the ones who are encountering my work for the first time, thank you for being here and for allowing me to share my ideas with you. Thank you for your questions, comments, shares, likes, purchases, and participation. This book would not have been possible without you.

Introduction

We all have stories that shape who we think we are. Our stories often have origins in our childhoods, and by the time we're adults, they are embedded in our subconscious beliefs. As we navigate through our lives, our stories continue to be influenced by our families, relationships, and societal and cultural factors.

You have many storylines that contribute to your sense of self. An example of a disempowering story could be that you're an underachiever. Perhaps you had a hard time in school, and now you believe that you are the disappointment of your family, and no one expects you to accomplish much. With this belief ingrained in your subconscious mind, you keep making decisions and repeating patterns that reinforce it. This story might cause you to avoid making a sincere effort because the belief that success is not possible for you is so solid in your mind.

The underachiever storyline can lead to a scarcity mindset that shows up in every aspect of your life—a fear of not being enough, not having enough, or doing enough. You might think that if you don't cling to what you have, you will lose it, and if you don't force what you want, you won't get it. This attachment to control can push away what you truly want, making your scarcity story seem true.

A disempowering story may feel like part of your identity, no less familiar than the city where you were born or whether you're right- or left-handed. You might tell yourself that you don't have what it takes to live the life you want to live. Maybe you feel limited by your past or destined to fall short in the future. Maybe someone told you that you're too much or not enough, and you believed them. These narratives are like spells that have been cast over us, influencing how we cope with the struggles and challenges in our lives. They diminish our self-concept, the language we use to describe ourselves, and our optimism about what's possible.

The truth is every experience you have is raw material that can be observed for its light and its shadow. You can believe that you are weakened by a situation or strengthened by it, and you will surely find evidence of what you choose to believe. You get to choose your perspective and assign your meaning. You can change your life by rewriting your story.

In *Story Work*, I highlight the creative connection between beliefs and actions and how this connection sets the stage for how our stories play out in our lives. I will show you how we can discover our stories by examining the beliefs that bring them to life. Together we will identify, reclaim, and reimagine the storylines that are not serving us so we can be empowered and not impaired by our experiences.

I know how hard it is to have a story in your bones, which seems like part of your identity. For years, I allowed my confusing childhood and bad decisions in young adulthood to define how I felt about the quality and worth of my life. My mental and physical health suffered from thinking this way. You will read about the stories I told myself that kept me from getting the help I needed. How I told myself that I was prewired for mental illness and that I'd spend the rest of my life waiting for my mind to betray me. How I didn't deserve happiness or abundance because I had made too many mistakes and disappointed myself and others too many times. How there was something broken inside that made me weak, lazy, selfish, and untrustworthy. These limiting beliefs showed up in my life as painful patterns, my life situations taking the form of the thoughts and feelings I was having on the inside. When you've thought about yourself a certain way for so long, to lose that identity can feel like losing your whole sense of self. In this book, you will receive guidance on how to release attachments to old stories and false identities.

I hope you were drawn to this book because you want to be more hopeful and intentional about the story you are telling with your life. You are seeking ways to overcome the doubts and insecurities that have restricted your path in the past. You are longing to disprove the tall tales you've believed about what you can do and who you can be. You want to expand your thinking to reimagine who you are and who you can become. You desire to take up space and add your true colors to the world. Despite these aspirations, your old stories may get in the way. My intention with this book is to show you creative ways to find new perspectives and discover what story you truly want your life to tell.

In the following pages, I share my personal stories and the reframing I've done in the past fifteen years, releasing old stories to develop new ways of thinking. *Story Work* will help you look at your life experiences with fresh eyes, feel more empowered to embrace your truth, and live your life in alignment with what moves you. You will walk away from this book knowing that you don't have to resign yourself to a lifetime of struggle and inner conflict. Even if you are navigating difficult long-term circumstances, it's possible to find purpose and thrive.

The Origins of Story Work

Story work is the term I use to describe the approach to self-discovery and storytelling that I teach in workshops. It involves recalling, reclaiming, and reimagining the stories of our lives through journaling exercises and cathartic storytelling. I didn't know what I was doing then, but this approach started taking shape in 2016 when I got intentional about journaling about my childhood and coming-of-age years. I experimented with journaling prompts and exercises to identify which memories to write about, with the present being a portal to the past. For example, a self-discovery prompt might be: *Where in your life do you currently feel like you're hiding?* Then the storytelling prompt would be: *Write a memory about the first time you remember hiding something about yourself.* I started making lists of key moments that were coming up through the exercises and writing down everything I could recall about each one. This process revealed beginnings and endings, turning points, peaks and valleys, breakdowns and breakthroughs, all begging me to write about them. This process turned avoidance into curiosity, and I found that my unexplored memories held wisdom for me. While there's so much about my past that I couldn't remember, I found that when I started with an object, a moment, a feeling, then gently, little by little, the detail bloomed into more. There was a particular memory that showed me the healing power of hindsight wisdom, which became a key part of my story work approach.

While I was growing up, my mother kept my evenings and weekends occupied with plenty of extracurricular activities, and I was rarely allowed to go to the mall, football games, and dances like many of my friends. In my early teens, I wanted to quit some of my activities, particularly dance classes, so I could spend more time hanging out. My mother and I disagreed on this. One day, she bought a canvas print of a white ballerina, colored in the skin with a brown crayon to make the ballerina look Black, and hung the canvas on my bedroom wall. I remember the big reveal: my mother pulling me into the room, flourishing her hands at her artwork as if to say, "Ta-da!"—her smile wide and her eyes bright with the joy of a child who just handed you a plastic plate of food prepared in their toy kitchen. I was embarrassed because the canvas looked as chaotic as my mother's behavior was at the time, and I didn't know how I would explain this spectacle to friends when they came over.

Before I revisited this memory in my thirties, I threw the Crayola ballerina into the same corner of my mind where I kept memories of my mother causing a scene or accusing me of doing bizarre and hurtful things. But hindsight revealed that this was different. This was a mother trying to inspire her daughter. A mother who put her daughter in ballet classes at three years old; who spent years driving her back and forth to dance classes multiple nights a week; who spent thousands of dollars on tuition, costumes, and gear; and who attended every recital. A mother who wanted to remind her daughter of their shared love of the arts, albeit in a makeshift, quirky way. This was a mother who didn't want her daughter to get distracted by boys and social life and lose sight of her goals and dreams. How could I not have seen that?

She did the best she could living with mental illness, undiagnosed and untreated, while trying to mother me. Using wisdom gained from hindsight, I was able to uncover a healing narrative, glean insight from the situation instead of angst, and use that interpretation to channel gratitude and understanding. One memory at a time, I continued writing about my life like I was digging for gold, and this transformed the way I interpreted my personal history.

Story work offers pathways to explore the stories that live inside of you. By honoring your experiences with curiosity instead of criticism, your story becomes a source of wisdom and guidance. From this practice, I created workshops, courses, and guided journals on self-care and self-inquiry. As I was developing the idea for this book, I thought about a name for this method, this combination of self-discovery and storytelling, inner work, and reclaiming your story. I landed on the term *story work*, which captures the alchemy of what it takes to turn your experiences into creative material that you can use to reclaim your past, present, and future.

I am not the first to use the term *story work* to describe a process of learning and finding meaning through life stories.

Q'um Q'um Xiiem, which means *strong, clear water,* also known as Dr. Jo-ann Archibald, is an Indigenous scholar, author, and pioneer in the advancement of Indigenous education. She learned about the important role of stories from Coast Salish Elders and other Indigenous storytellers who taught that stories can guide the development of our heart, mind, body, and spirit. Through the elders' guidance and mentorship, she developed a way to celebrate and understand the sacred power of Indigenous stories and named this methodology *Indigenous story work.*

Built on fundamental principles of place-based knowing, learning through hands-on experience, and the role of elders as cultural knowledge holders, the practice that holds it all together is storytelling. Through the oral tradition of storytelling and the mentorship and guidance of elders, Indigenous story work is a vehicle for intergenerational knowledge.

In social work, the term *life story work* is used to describe an intervention with children and adults to help them identify with their past, present, and future. A concept that has dated back to the 1960s, it is primarily used with children who will be adopted and older adults as part of reminiscence therapies for Alzheimer's and other cognitive diseases.

For children who are in long-term custodial or adoptive care, life story work may include working with social workers, who often have the most accurate information about the person's background, as well as day-to-day caregivers who have access to daily events, milestones, and achievements. The system supports children in understanding feelings associated with their past and connecting the dots to their current feelings and behaviors. Life story work can take place through interactive discussion and storytelling, as well as creating a tangible life story book that answers questions the child may have in the future about their history.

The American Psychological Association defines reminiscence therapy as "the use of life histories—written, oral, or both—to improve psychological well-being." This form of life story work helps elderly patients recall and reexperience events to identify continuity between the past and the present and find meaning and worth in their lives. It has also been found to be beneficial as a therapeutic tool for family members to assist in reviewing the person's life and enabling them to remember the person prior to the onset of cognitive decline. It may include creating visual tools to trigger their memories of past events, as well as oral storytelling in group therapy environments.

There may be more approaches that use the term *story work* out there that I don't know about, but the connective tissue is the idea that storytelling heals. Across cultures and history, stories have allowed us to offer up our humanity as a gift. They serve as entry points for deeper empathy and connection, and they make the personal universal by bridging the gap between individual and collective experience. We all have parts of ourselves that we've kept hidden, and this book's purpose is to develop healing narratives that help us navigate these parts with more hope and a broader vision.

How to Read This Book

Do you need to have a journaling habit or consider yourself a writer to get the most out of this book? Absolutely not. *Story Work* is for anyone who is interested in utilizing the healing power of storytelling.

Each chapter includes creative material from my own life. I'm sharing personal reflections to bring you into my experience and show you how I've turned around my defeated stories. I am doing this work right with you, asking the questions, and mining my material. I offer my truths and circumstances as I remember them and as I now see them, followed by the narrative story work I've done to give those truths an empowering and hopeful meaning. Each personal story expands into a broader reflection of what that moment could mean and how to use creative thinking to explore the possibilities. At the end of each chapter, I provide a reflection exercise to help you take stock of your creative material, reclaim your narratives, and apply the concepts to your life. With references from literature, philosophy, science, and spirituality, the concepts I share come from my personal and professional experience and research on writing as a tool for healing, personal growth, and creative expression.

Vulnerability is contagious. By witnessing my story and the way I transformed it, you will come away with tools for your self-discovery. I recommend reading the chapters in order because they are intentionally sequenced to start with your origins and expand from there. You may choose to read through the whole book before working on the reflection exercises at the end of each chapter, or you may choose to work on the reflection exercises as you go. That's totally up to you. I encourage you to pace yourself and take your time so you can absorb and reflect as you read. This book will trigger memories and reflections from your past, and sometimes this will be painful, but it will also be enlightening and eye-opening as you come out the other side of it with new tools. I recommend preparing yourself by having someone to talk to if the book brings up challenging memories. This could be a mental health professional or a trusted friend or loved one. When uncomfortable emotions come up, nurture yourself by taking a break. Connect with your support network. Shift your attention from the discomfort to the personal growth and self-ownership that are blooming from it. Take your time and become your own safe space to be honest and gracious with yourself. To help you do that, keep these thoughts in mind:

- Courage starts in solitude when we dare to tell ourselves the truth and explore what's going on in our inner worlds.
- We risk the initial discomfort of self-discovery for the hope and meaning it provides.

- Putting your feelings down on the page helps you be honest with yourself and experience the healing power of creative expression.
- The discomfort of vulnerability is a necessary part of growth, and when you change your relationship with it, the discomfort gives way to expansion.

As Toni Morrison said during her Wellesley College Commencement address in 2004, "Your life is already artful—waiting, just waiting, for you to make it art." Let's begin.

Part I

Roots and Origins

That is the way it is with a wound. The wound begins to close in on itself, to protect what is hurting so much. And once it is closed, you no longer see what is underneath, what started the pain.

—Amy Tan

Chapter One

Months Turned into Years

The last time my mother came to visit, she arrived smelling of cigarettes, coffee, and Blue Magic hair grease. I inhaled her familiar fragrance as I hugged her, then loaded up her things and drove the forty minutes from the Baltimore bus station back to my place in Silver Spring, Maryland, where I lived with my partner and two kids. She would be our guest for the next week.

At home, we were greeted by a blue postcard on the door saying the water had been turned off. My stomach tightened, and my mind raced as I read the terms. In bold black letters, the note said that even if we paid the bill immediately, the water company would not come out to turn the water back on until the next business day, two whole days away. I knew my mother would not do well with this: The problem had nothing to do with her, but she wouldn't see it that way. In her eyes, trouble followed her. Someone was always after her, watching and plotting. Her paranoia gave her no rest, and I had no rest when I was with her.

"I have to go," she said as I put the key in the front door. "They don't want me here."

As we stepped into the house, my seven-year-old son and three-year-old daughter ran straight through the kitchen into the family room for their toys, oblivious to the inconvenience and rising tension.

Standing in the kitchen near the front door, my mom said, "I have enough money to get a hotel. Is there one close by? If I'm not here, they'll leave you alone."

Shaking my head no before she could finish her sentence, I said, "It's okay, Mom. Sit down. Let me get you something to drink."

She wouldn't sit down or get comfortable, and she kept her oversized purse, loaded with presents for the kids, on her shoulder. Moving the purse from side to side, she paced the room talking to herself, maybe talking to me—I couldn't be sure because she wouldn't look at me or respond to anything I said. I recognized the signs of her spiraling. Never mind the nuisance of going two days without running water or the shame of forgetting to pay the bill; the real crisis here was my mother having an episode before the visit could even begin.

"Mom? *Mom.* No way, you just got here. We'll figure this out. Mom, can you get the kids settled while I make a couple of calls?" Speaking through the tightness of my throat, I used a soothing tone. Each time I said *Mom*, I attempted to make gentle eye contact.

When I mentioned the kids, she met my eyes and returned to me, as I'd seen her do so many times before, like a trance was lifted. She took her purse off her shoulder and walked into the family room, holding the straps open to reveal the goodies inside.

"Look what Grandma has for you!" she exclaimed.

I melted into the kitchen chair, realizing that I'd barely been breathing. But I'd stayed calm. I'd remembered how to handle her. I still believed that if I tried hard enough, I could outsmart the voices in her head and make her feel safe.

Deliverance

My memories of my mother's psychotic episodes begin at around the age of nine. She would come in my room in the middle of the night and sit on the edge of my twin Strawberry Shortcake bed, sometimes calm and trancelike, sometimes yelling. She'd tell me about the evil things I'd done that day—delusions that dirtied my mind and broke my heart. Before this shift, I believed I was her favorite person in the world, so I knew something had gone wrong. I wanted to please her and tried to do everything right so she would stop being suspicious of me.

One morning, I sleepily walked in on my father using the bathroom, and she accused me of trying to seduce him. Shame became a vine, creeping up my legs; wrapping around my stomach, chest, and throat; stealing my voice. When she told me I was a bad girl with bad intentions, I believed her. I got used to walking on eggshells and being at fault and not understanding why. Anxiety took root and grew, the seeds watered with every accusation, as I struggled to determine what was real and what was not. After that defining moment, I felt an unwanted presence in my mind, separating me from my innocence. Hopelessness settled into my bones.

I went through adolescence perplexed at my mother's erratic behavior and my father's gaping silence. Shame hardened into resentment. I held them both responsible for keeping me in the dark, for giving me so much to hide and lie about. Mom was tormented by something—I could see it in her eyes and hear it in her voice—but I knew nothing about mental illness, and they provided no explanation of what was happening.

In this environment, I learned how to internalize my questions and come to my own conclusions. When my mother accused me of flirting with my father, I believed there was something unnatural in me that I wasn't aware of and couldn't control. When my father did not intervene or speak up for me, I decided I couldn't expect this kind of help from anyone, and later I would go on to choose men who didn't know how to support me emotionally. There was no room for me to express anger or indignation, to have my feelings acknowledged. So I became hypervigilant about managing my parents' limitations and expectations.

If I walked into the kitchen to find that my dad left the milk on the counter, I put it in the fridge so my mother wouldn't accuse him of trying to poison her, starting an argument and ruining the day. When my mother told me that my dad's side of the family was stalking her and she didn't want me to see them, I didn't try to change her mind. I heard the sadness in my dad's voice when he returned from gatherings at Nana's saying, "Everyone asked about you," but I tried not to dwell on it because it was my burden and responsibility to keep the peace in our home in whatever way I could. It is not out of the ordinary for parents with mental illness to put their children in situations that make them feel helpless, overwhelmed, and unprotected. Most of these circumstances occur within the intimacy of the home, and the children are taught that what happens behind closed doors stays there.

Soon after I graduated from high school, our family home in Pittsburgh was foreclosed, and my mother moved to New York City for what she called a fresh start. By then, my parents were separated, and my father had moved in with his mother, Nana, whose health was declining. When my mother moved, she stayed with her favorite cousin, CoCo, in Long Island and got a job working as a receptionist in the city. I don't know what happened at that job, but one day my mother called to tell me she would no longer be working there.

"They let me go today and told me I should get a psych evaluation."

"Wait, what? Why? What happened?" My stomach started churning.

"They said that if I'm diagnosed with a mental illness, I could be eligible for disability benefits. That means I won't have to work anymore!"

I didn't know what to do with this information, but I couldn't match her joy. It was the late '90s, and I was sitting in my dorm room at Morgan State University in Baltimore. I had never once heard my mother or any other adult in my family talk about psychological evaluations or diagnoses. I knew nothing about mental illness and disability benefits, but

I could imagine the type of behavior that led to this development. Was she accusing her coworkers of following her home and watching her through the windows? Was she talking to herself in a loud voice at her desk? Maybe she was covering her eyes with her hands when she spoke to people to prevent them from raping her with their eyes, something she'd warned me about repeatedly. Her symptoms had intensified through years of secrecy and avoidance, presenting one hallucination after another, distorting one relationship after the next. She was already estranged from her old friends, younger brother, and older sister and rarely spoke to her mother and father. It was only a matter of time before she wouldn't be able to work anymore. After the termination, she continued to stay with her cousin for a while, but eventually, CoCo insisted she get help, and my mother left.

Later, she was diagnosed with schizophrenia—a mental illness characterized by hallucinations, delusions, and disordered thinking that impairs one's perception of reality. What the doctors called a disorder, my mother considered a deliverance. Schizophrenia provided access to a place where she felt protected, gifted with an ability to sense danger that others couldn't. With this perspective, she was not interested in treatment or medication.

She seemed happy about retiring, which is what she called it, but she believed the diagnosis turned a gift into a threat and made her more vulnerable to the Brownies, a secret organization that was persecuting her. They were everywhere, she said. Now that she was in the system, it was easier for them to get to her, she said. They were blocking her from getting a job, she said. Blocking her from finding a place to live. Forcing her onto the streets. She believed that her family members were all under the influence of the Brownies, my father and me included.

She continued to live in New York alone, moving from shelter to shelter. When she attended my college graduation in

2000, she brought her friend Sheila, whom she met in one of her temporary living situations. They were both part of a government program where they were waiting for permanent subsidized housing to come through. I remember being perplexed and overwhelmed by the way my mom explained things. She blended reality with delusion so seamlessly that it was hard to know what was real and what was not. I wanted her to get treatment, but it upset her when I brought it up. She expected me to cooperate—to entertain her delusions, to plead guilty to her accusations, to ignore my common sense—because that is how I'd responded to her as a little girl. As a young woman, I couldn't give her that surrender anymore.

Frustrated, I searched myself and found self-preservation where I thought I'd find loyalty. I wanted my mother in my life, not this untreated disorder that turned her into someone else. My fear, my haunting regret, is that my family and I didn't try hard enough to understand her condition, to address it directly, to get help, to put an end to the denial and the mystery. Perhaps we could have forced her to get help. Sam, my older brother from my mom's first marriage, was occupied with raising his own young family and was silent on the subject as well. We'd both been conditioned to float with the stream. We never talked about her diagnosis. Instead, we sat in our denial and watched, and when we couldn't watch anymore, we looked the other way.

I knew I couldn't cure her or force her to admit she wasn't well, and I didn't blame myself for that, but I hated myself for not being actively involved in her life, for being conditional. Guilt told me that I should find a way to stay close to her and watch over her. Instead, I rarely saw my mother—and when I did, I was anxious to get away. Without realizing it, I emulated the adults in my life by choosing avoidance over presence. I struggled with protecting myself and protecting her, ultimately failing at both.

In my mind, if I were a better woman, a worthy daughter, I would have persisted, and I would not have given up until I got her the care she needed. I would have held her hand even when she tried to pull away. Instead, I limited our in-person visits throughout college. Letters and phone calls kept us from drifting apart through my twenties. She took a Greyhound bus from New York to Baltimore when I had my first child in 2002 and again when I had my second in 2005. She washed dishes, cooked meals, and changed diapers, helping me in those first few days of shell shock after giving birth, just like many of us hope our mothers will do. Those are my last memories of feeling taken care of and held by her, and I remember the sweet melancholy of watching her care for her grandchildren. She was at her best on those visits. Maybe she was medicated, but I never saw her take anything. When she was with us, we tried to merge our worlds without too much conflict, which means I didn't ask questions I knew would upset her. It was on one such visit in 2008 when we came home to the blue note on the door.

Magical Thinking

Throughout the waterless weekend, I looked forward to Monday so I could prove the voices wrong. My partner and I would pay the bill, and all would be well. My mother would see that the voices in her head were wrong. She would mumble something about being off her medication, and she'd ask me to take her to the doctor the very next day. We'd have a heart-to-heart over coffee, and I'd even let her smoke a cigarette right there in my house to help her relax. I would tell her how much I worry about her and want her to get help. The trance would lift, and there would be a moment of clarity, a brightness in her eyes, and she'd see me as her daughter, not a threat. Feeling seen for the first time, I would confess that I have scary thoughts that come from a place I can't control. I'd ask her when—as a girl? as a woman?—did she know that her mind was wired differently. When did she start hearing voices, and how did she know they weren't hers? She would tell me about the voices and what it's like to see and hear things that others can't. I would learn how to enter her world without losing myself there. We would cry, and my prayers would be answered.

But my magical thinking didn't work. In reality, we slowly waded through the weekend and the rest of the visit. I paid the bill, the water flowed, but it didn't matter because there were already new threats circling her mind. She claimed my neighbor shot lasers at her through the kitchen window one morning.

"I knew I should have stayed away from the window! I don't think I was hit, but you can never be sure."

According to her, someone kept moving her bag and filling it with open safety pins that she would leave in piles on my bedroom dresser as proof. This was reminiscent of my childhood when she often accused me of putting open safety pins in her bag so she would prick herself.

"I don't know if you're up to your old tricks or if you put someone else up to it, but it's not going to work. I can tell when someone touches my things."

She heard an echo when she spoke, so the house must have been bugged.

"The Brownies in Maryland must be excited that I'm here. They've pulled out all the stops, haven't they?"

I changed the subject. I distracted her. I used the kids as buffers for me and mood stabilizers for her. A knot developed in my stomach that did not unravel until it was time for her to go. We returned to the Baltimore bus station seven days after discovering the blue note on the door. As usual, I was both relieved and terrified to see her go. I told her I loved her and I'd talk to her soon, but deep down, I knew I needed some space. Maybe I imagined it, but she seemed exhausted too. She wouldn't look me directly in the eyes. She wouldn't allow me to stay and wait with her. With a wide smile, a flicker of her former self, she assured me she was fine and told me to go home. Pulling her close, I inhaled her once more before I left with the same frustration I'd come with, wishing we could help each other but not knowing how.

After that visit, her phone calls and letters continued, but I was weary of her and slow to respond. She left long voicemail messages, some about gardening and shopping, others about government conspiracies against her, secret organizations, and black magic. My responses were lukewarm at best. I didn't want the knot to return, the stomach tightening, the fear of the next episode. Then, without warning, the calls and letters stopped.

At first, I breathed easier. When my mother made no contact for one year, two years, three years, and longer, I didn't hunt her down. I spoke to God about her. I prayed for her to be well and safe, and I prayed for her to stay away. I was certain that her absence would bring me peace. But as the years added up, I became painfully anxious, more and more afraid for her, dreading the consequences of letting her slip away.

When I got home from the bus station that night, I poured myself a glass of wine and reviewed the past few days in my mind. It occurred to me that maybe she was tired of trying too. Perhaps she'd come for this visit with the same hopes I had, the same longing to be heard, if not understood. Maybe she came to remind me that, while her reality had departed from mine, it was still quite real to her, that she was where she wanted to be—in a world that became a refuge for her when this one stopped making sense.

Closed Doors

As I was growing up in a Black, middle-class family in the '80s, if there was any discussion about mental illness around me, it was whispered. Physical ailments were discussed openly, with candor and even humor. My grandmother used to warn me that if I continued to put heaping spoonfuls of sugar in my cereal, I would end up with diabetes, unable to have any sweets at all. The adults would sit around and swap stories about their symptoms, medications, and side effects, admitting to pain in their bodies but never in their minds.

Mental health issues were sent to church and kept behind closed doors. No one sat around the card table chatting about their anxiety attacks, hallucinations, or suicidal thoughts. In the Black community, we already had enough cards stacked against us; the worst thing you could do was make yourself look unstable. What I learned, watching and listening to my family, is that our people didn't have the luxury of being of unsound mind. We had to stay sharp and suppress our pain and emotions to survive.

What my parents didn't teach me, and what they were never taught, is that mental illness is not a weakness, a character flaw, or a punishment from God. The stigma comes from misinformation and fear because when we don't understand a thing, we create assumptions around it. And when we can't control a thing, we lie and cover it up. As a result of this pressure to look unbreakable, mental illness is a hidden chaos in many homes.

According to research, the children of mentally ill parents have unique emotional hardships and face an increased risk of developing mental health disorders. When the parent's illness creates a disturbance in the home but is not openly acknowledged and explained, the impact is even more troubling. Many of us grew up in a prolonged state of distress that triggered instabilities of our own. There are parts of us that never felt safe, stories we were too afraid to tell. As children, we were disoriented and confused because we didn't understand our parents' behavior or how to respond to it. We had to master the art of keeping secrets.

My mother started accusing me of flirting with my dad when I was too young to even understand what that meant.

I didn't know what I was doing wrong, so I stopped being myself with him. No more playing footsie with him under the kitchen table. No more playing Go Fish on my parents' bed after school. For a while, I looked at the floor when I spoke to him. Her mind was telling her things that were scary, twisted, and untrue, so I kept my distance to avoid her sick translation of us. Confronting the loss of my dad's company and my mother's trust—plus believing that it was my fault—bent my reality completely out of shape. I would spend most of my adolescence and young adult life trying to prove to the world (and myself) that it didn't.

Strong Enough

That visit was the beginning of a long-term estrangement from my mother. Months turned into years as I made silent promises to reconnect with her once I got my life together. Once I got a handle on my emotional instabilities, I'd be strong enough to handle hers. Once I stopped crying every day, stopped waiting to hear voices and lose touch with reality. Once I stopped being easily triggered and manipulated. Once I got braver, stronger, I'd suddenly have the superpowers needed to support her. I thought the courage I needed to reenter her world would come on its own with time.

I couldn't find the words to explain why I chose not to stay in contact with her, so I didn't talk about it. The guilt I held in my gut, throat, and the shadows of my mind became unbearable. The thought of her being in my life brought waves of dread and visions of drowning. Imagine that you are not a strong swimmer, and you're in deep water with someone who is panicking and refuses to be helped. You try to calm them, and they scream louder, thrash wilder. Every time you wrap your arms around them, they pull you under. They don't mean to; they don't consciously want to hurt you, but they can't help themselves. This is what it was like with her. She refused treatment. She refused counseling. She went in and out of delusional states. How could I subject my children to that kind of chaos?

But her absence haunted me every day, and I mourned the relationship we lost. Her absence took up space at all my kids' birthday celebrations, recitals, and milestones. I saw women who looked like her, all the different versions of her that I'd known—everywhere. At flea markets, I saw her (and me) in mother-daughter pairs, drooling over handmade jewelry and art. In the library, I saw her in middle-aged, dark-skinned women, hair pulled up in a fuzzy bun and glasses on the tip of her nose, checking out a stack of books. I saw her on the street, in every Black woman shrouded in layers of mismatched clothing, carrying a bag or cart with her whole life in it. I had no way of knowing if she was taking care of herself, if she was safe and secure. Staying away did not free me from anything. I carried sadness around like a ticking time bomb that could explode at any moment. By avoiding my mother's burden, I had created my own.

Life doesn't stop for us when we are in deep water and sinking, so we struggle to keep our heads above the water, and we tell ourselves that we will deal with what's pulling us under the surface as soon as we can. As soon as there's time, space, energy, money—a miracle, perhaps, a divine shift, maybe even a disruption. But we don't need to wait for a miracle to transform our lives. Each of us is on an inner journey that is reflected outwardly. In her first published book, *D. H. Lawrence: An Unprofessional Study*, Anaïs Nin tells us that a day will come when the risk to remain tight in the bud becomes more painful than the risk it takes to blossom.

She goes on to say, "Life is a process of becoming, a combination of states we have to go through. Where people fail is that they wish to elect a state and remain in it. This is a kind of death." We can find courage for the new states that wait for us when we recognize that every challenge hides an opportunity. Our wounds lead us to look within ourselves, to face our inner questions and sit in the discomfort of answering them. Even when our discoveries are painful, finding themes and patterns has a healing effect. The alternative is to look at our lives and only see scars that will never heal.

Losing my relationship with my mother would ultimately send me on a journey where I had to get lost to find my way back to my authentic self. The perfect time to face it never came, and I never got the magical amount of space, energy, or money that I thought would make it all make sense. But several years later, a quiet miracle did occur, a shift in my perspective that changed the story I was telling myself about who I am and who I could become.

Reflection: Living the Questions

> *Be patient toward all that is unsolved in your heart and try to love the questions themselves, like locked rooms and like books that are now written in a very foreign tongue. Do not now seek the answers, which cannot be given you because you would not be able to live them. And the point is, to live everything. Live the questions now. Perhaps you will then gradually, without noticing it, live along some distant day into the answer.*
>
> —Rainer Maria Rilke

The journey of self-discovery begins when we turn to face our inner questions. They are often questions that life keeps asking, presenting to us, in a myriad of ways. Even if you don't have the answers, brave questions awaken bravery. Honest questions awaken honesty. Questions reveal the underlying needs, fears, doubts, and desires that live in your subconscious mind. When you ask a question, you start paying attention to life, looking for it to answer that question, to offer you a clue. The question increases your receptivity and connects you to invisible, universal support. Open-ended questions help us begin thinking in new ways, which helps us discover answers that were always inside of us but we couldn't access before.

When you question your thoughts, beliefs, and assumptions, you begin to notice inner conflicts and areas of ambiguity. Do your thoughts always align with who you are? Do they always align with who you want to be? Of course not. We have subconscious limiting beliefs—stories we tell ourselves that hold us back from walking in our truths and living our most authentic lives. We make our limiting beliefs a reality when we align our actions with them. For example, when I believed that I was not strong enough to face my mother's illness, I didn't take steps to educate myself or get involved in her care. I chose avoidance. The avoidance led to guilt and shame. The guilt and shame led to more limiting beliefs like not only am I not strong enough, but I'm also selfish and useless.

We should question any story or inner narrative that leaves no room for hope. You can practice gentle self-observation by focusing on a limiting belief about your life choices and circumstances. A few examples are *I'm bad with money. I have a disability or difference that keeps me from pursuing my dreams. I'll never find a partner. Everyone abandons me. It's too late for me to turn my life around.* Choose one belief that is leading you to a defeated story about the possibilities for your life, then ask yourself a series of questions:

- Why do I have this belief?
- How does this belief make me feel empowered or disempowered?
- What facts do I have to support this belief?
- How does this belief affect my feelings, thoughts, and behavior?
- What assumptions am I making?

- What kind of evidence would change this belief?
- Does this belief align with my values?
- What other beliefs could be true that do align with my values?

What other questions come to mind for you? Think about the questions that life has been trying to get you to notice. It could be something that the minister says at church. A conversation you overhear while waiting in line. A social media post that shows up on your timeline. If we're not ready to be honest with ourselves and acknowledge these messages, we will miss them. You will see as you continue reading that when I began to believe I could not only acknowledge and survive my questions but also thrive in them, the way I felt about my story started to change, and hopefully, yours will too.

Chapter Two

Smile and Wave

In a quiet suburb in Montgomery County, Maryland, the sun is setting on a humid summer day. There's a swarm of sweaty men playing soccer on the field. A blur of kids running, swinging, and bouncing across the playground. The scene is like an ad for prescription drugs where everyone is happy, thriving, and moving in slow motion. As I turn left into our neighborhood, the streetlights illuminate, welcoming us back. Driving down the tree-lined road, I see families walking dogs and riding bikes in the fading light.

I smile and wave at the familiar faces and wonder about their lives at home, a habit I developed when I was a little girl trying to make sense of my own family life. Back then, my parents and I had secrets behind our smiles and waves. I dreamed of one day having a different kind of home where no one walked around on eggshells, afraid to say or do the wrong thing at the wrong time. Now, glancing at the back seat at my own three kids, I worry that I've fallen short of that goal.

My smile fades. There is a part of me that struggles with the illusion of it all, the way society focuses on appearances. We all smile and wave, but you never know what people are dealing with under the surface. At this moment, I look like a mom driving home with my kids, but inside I'm wondering if I am being the mother I'd hoped to be. I'm taking in the field, the playground, the road in front of me, but I'm thinking about whether or not I'm giving them the accountability and open communication that I didn't receive. Their questions echo in my mind—*Can we have a family movie night with all of us together, including Daddy this time? Why were you yelling at each other last night? Sometimes we only see you in the morning and when it's time to go to bed. Why do you have to work so much?*—questions I struggled to answer for myself, let alone find age-appropriate answers for my kids. In my childhood, I held myself responsible for managing my parents' limitations, and I did the same thing when I became a mother, protecting my kids from my and their father's limitations instead of addressing them.

Do you have inconvenient questions that linger in the back of your mind? Questions that live in the eyes of the ones you love? Tangles that wake you up at 3:00 a.m. asking to be unraveled or that you have to push aside to get through the demands of the day? The parts of your life that you don't show on social media or chat about with coworkers. The disappointments you are carrying and the promises you are breaking. They sit behind our smiles and waves, and we try not to let those thoughts suck us in and pull us down. What are you carrying? How is it affecting you?

As I pull into our numbered parking spot in front of our town house, I bring myself back to the present moment. To wake up the kids, I grab each one of their golden-brown legs and give them a shake. Nate, the oldest, wakes up first and pushes Rayna's head off his shoulder. Unfazed, she lets her head fall back onto the seat. Stuck in the middle by both age and position, she will be the hardest to get moving. Sienna sits up in her car seat, stretching and rubbing her eyes. I wish they were still small enough to carry inside without waking them. They'll be up late now. Their needy years are flying by, but for now, they still rely on me to tell them what to do next. *Who gets in the shower first? What do we have to eat? Where do I put this bag?* Their dependence reminds me that I have a temporary window of opportunity to shape them in this way.

Not that long ago, I was a child with two imperfect parents doing their best to provide a loving home for me. When I was at the peak of my childhood innocence, my mother was my best friend, my father was my hero, and we looked like a normal family. My dad was a gentle giant who single-handedly built a deck on the side of our suburban split-level home, along with flower beds, vegetable gardens, a swing and picnic table for our back patio and yard. Labors of love so my mother could have artful spaces to entertain, read, and grow whatever plant life she wanted within a gated area where I could safely play. A man of few words, his actions spoke for him.

If my dad's love language was service, then let's say my mom's love language was culture. I remember hot summer days when her legs stretched bare and brown before me as she led me through my hand-holding years in the early '80s. I scurried behind her to churches, temples, museums, libraries, plays, and art festivals. She acted out scenes from *The Color Purple* with me, volunteered at my school, and introduced me to God. She was my safe place, but as I grew into adolescence, she became suspicious of me, and life as I knew it changed.

I didn't think about the fact that my time with them would be limited. It certainly never occurred to me that I would lose them mentally before I lost them physically, but as my friend had pointed out earlier that day, that's essentially what happened.

The Question

A few hours before getting home, my children and I had stopped by a friend's house to say hello after back-to-back practices and errands. With their inviting yard and house full of kids, this was the perfect way to end a hot summer day. I could have some grown-up conversation while the kids blew off whatever steam they had left.

Michelle is known and loved for her unfiltered honesty. She doesn't shrink from uncomfortable questions, and she reads people like a sailor reads the wind. We were sitting on her porch talking about the differences between our parents' generation and our own while the little ones ran wild in the yard. Already disheveled and irrational from being out all day, the kids were in rare form, running into each other and falling down laughing. I knew it wouldn't be long before someone's tears would end the visit and send us home.

I kept a close eye on them as my friend and I talked about growing up in the '80s. We declared that we would do things differently than our parents by having open communication with our kids. We both recall getting our menstrual cycles with little explanation or direction and learning about sex from school friends and Cinemax. We both remember traumatic things happening and no one explaining anything to us. We were both taught that you don't put your family secrets out in the street, and you don't get involved in grown folks' conversations. These were standard rules in our Black American childhood homes. We cackled as we imitated the faces our parents made to shush us when we said too much in public.

That's when my mind began to drift. The conversation continued on the surface, but underneath, deeper questions were forming: *At what point does protecting your privacy become pretending, performing, and denying reality? At what point does privacy become silenced truth and does silenced truth become erased history? Am I doing things differently from my parents like I wanted to?* Michelle's next question pulled me back into the moment.

She said, "Both of your parents sort of faded away slowly, didn't they? That must be a lot to carry."

As the words came out of her mouth, my heart jumped in my chest; the ground swayed under my feet, reminding me of the time I was ten floors up during an earthquake. I took a deep breath to ease the butterflies her question set in motion.

She waited patiently, holding time still for me. She didn't change the subject or retract the question. I looked at her and said, "I never thought of it that way, but yeah. They did."

By now, it had been about six years since I'd spoken to my mother. I had an address for her in Florida, but I'd never visited her there. By now, dementia had taken away my father's personality, his ability to walk, talk, and smile with that sparkle in his eyes. In both instances, for different reasons, my parents had faded away from me slowly. Her question triggered the little girl in me who was still waiting for her parents to sit her down and explain what happened and what to do without them.

My time with my parents was cut short by illness, avoidance, and silence, and it hurts when I think about the time we lost. Every time I do think about it, every time someone asks if I've heard from my mom, every time I allow myself to consider if my choices make me a bad person, the ground sways under my feet, and the world is unsteady. I was living with an underground of unsaid words and unasked questions, an earthquake waiting to happen.

Rearview Mirror

I was on autopilot for the rest of the conversation, eager to be alone with my thoughts for the drive home. We got through the hugging and kissing goodbye without incident, despite the kids' complete delirium at that point.

As I pull out of my friend's neighborhood, I catch my youngest watching me in the rearview mirror from her sticky throne in the back seat.

"Mommy, relax your face," she says.

She's affected by the moods and energies around her, just like I am. When she sees my forehead wrinkled, eyebrows furled, and lips pressed tightly together, she assumes something is wrong. I make a silly face in the mirror to assure her there's nothing to worry about.

I remember when I was the one in the back seat, watching my mother's faces and gestures, trying to predict her moods. Riding along, I would study the houses we passed and the families inside, wondering if they had secrets like us. *Are those smiling people with the bikes and toys sprinkled across the lawn as happy as they look? Does that woman hear angry voices in her head that tell her awful things? Do other mothers accuse their daughters of lusting after their fathers?*

By the time I was a teenager, my mother's bizarre accusations were routine and expected. She regularly accused my father of flirting with me, my sister from his first marriage, other family members, friends, bank tellers, and waitresses. She was wary of the neighbors, convinced they were watching her and coming into our house when we weren't there. Coworkers were sabotaging her, the people at church were invading her dreams, and strangers on the street were putting thoughts into her head. As time went on, she became more unpredictable—hearing voices I couldn't hear, seeing things I couldn't see, fading away from my reality as my questions went unasked and unanswered.

My father didn't address what was happening, and my mother wouldn't admit that anything was wrong. Watching their example, I'd grown up swallowing my confusion and living in denial of what I saw and felt and knew. Comforting myself with the thought that as long as we looked like a normal family, the world would not end. Now, as a mother facing my children's hard questions, I had more understanding of how difficult it must have been for my parents to navigate their challenges while trying to shelter me. I started thinking about them as humans and not just parents whose lives were solely in service of raising me.

The Silent Generation

My parents were part of what is called the Silent Generation, the era preceding the baby boomers. Coming up under the influence of Jim Crow laws and pervasive racial oppression, the aftermath of the Great Depression, World War II, and the threat of the Korean War, they were called the "Silents" because the youths of this era were taught to be seen and not heard, to work hard and not complain. Secrecy was a survival tactic, and protecting family was everything. In the Black community, this notion of silence was even more crucial to avoid unwanted attention and the persecution that came with it.

Even my mother somehow stayed true to these principles as her undiagnosed illness progressed. She'd leave disturbing voicemail messages on our church's answering machine in the middle of the night, accusing them of torturing her with black magic. Then she'd wake up the next day, put on her favorite dress, and attend all three services at church like nothing happened. My father carried on a relationship outside of his broken marriage for years and still came home every day, paid the bills, and maintained the appearance of a stable home. They showed me without telling me that secrets protect the family, and honest discussion threatens it.

In *Sisters of the Yam: Black Women and Self-Recovery*, bell hooks says,

> If illusions are valued more than reality, and Black children are taught how to skillfully create them even as they are simultaneously deprived of the means to face reality, they are being socialized to feel comfortable, at ease, only in situations where lying is taking place. They are being taught to exist in a state of denial. These psychic conditions lay the groundwork for mental stress, for mental illness. Dissimulation makes us dysfunctional. Since it encourages us to deny what we genuinely feel and experience, we lose our capacity to know who we really are and what we need and desire.

I've seen how the pain of unhealed family wounds passes through generations. As much as I wanted to create a healthy environment for my kids, I didn't know how to model it in real time. I only knew how to struggle in silence. They'd seen me lying in bed all weekend surrounded by piles of laundry and dirty dishes, sick with an invisible, unacknowledged illness, eyes red with self-medication and tears. Only to get up on Monday and go to work pressed and polished with no trace of the weekend's collapse. They'd heard me stretch reality to keep the peace and shush them when they spoke truths I couldn't face. Trained that kids don't need explanations, I compensated with hugs and kisses, hoping affection would heal their confusion. I told myself that if we looked like a normal family, the world would not end.

As I drove home through the familiar streets from my friend's house that day, I thought about how silence didn't protect our family, and it didn't keep my parents from fading away. What it did was create barriers that weakened our relationships, suppressed truths, and left me with a legacy of unanswered questions. After years of frustrating patterns, I allowed myself to acknowledge the resentment and shame I'd been carrying and how I was inadvertently continuing the generational patterns that created it. A voice inside of me said: *It's not too late. This pattern can still end with you.*

Seeds of Transformation

"Both of your parents sort of faded away slowly, didn't they?" I'm still reflecting on my friend's burning question as I settle the kids into bed that night. It came at the right time from the right place. She delivered it with love, and I was ready to receive it, to be changed by it. Was I wrong to distance myself from my mother? Should I have demanded more answers from my father? What could I have done differently? What could my parents have done differently? All the way home, my mind revisited these unanswerable questions, and the motion of the ride seemed to generate ideas almost as if a voice inside was answering me. In *Wired to Create: Unraveling the Gifts of the Creative Mind*, the authors describe insights as gifts from the unconscious mind. They quote decision-making expert Gary Klein in a 2013 interview with *Huffington Post*: "An insight is an unexpected shift in the way we understand things. It comes without warning. It's not something we think is going to happen and that's why it's unexpected. It feels like a gift and in fact it is."

Something has shifted. A certainty has settled over me. I still feel the shame, guilt, and regret, but there is also resolve. I don't want the topic of my parents to be a fault line anymore, an earthquake waiting to happen. I realize that by suppressing the pain all these years, I'd also been suppressing joy, insight, and wisdom that I could pass along to my kids. Instead of being ashamed of myself for how I'd handled things, I could share my honest truth as an expression of my humanity and the complexity that all humans face, one way or another. I'm realizing that while I can't change the past, I can change the meaning that I assign to how my parents' love and imperfections shaped me. I didn't always recognize their wisdom when I had access to it, but I could seek the counsel and comfort I crave from them by studying their lives and looking for the light. From this perspective, I could observe their lives just as I was beginning to observe my own—with curiosity and a desire to learn, instead of judgment.

Looking down at my kids' plump little faces in their beds, I hear words from Nikki Giovanni's poem "The Life I Led" come to me, and I offer a silent prayer that my son and daughters will one day be warmed by the life I tried to live. I find a resolution that gives me hope. In difficult moments when I'm tempted to choose silence or inaction, I can remember that I don't need all the answers, only the willingness to keep acknowledging the hard questions. Hard questions can help me make new choices: *Am I going to repeat this cycle, knowing the burden I am putting on my kids by doing so? How am I honoring what I've learned from my parents' choices?*

What new choices could come from *your* hard questions?

When our families are the source of great joy and great pain, there is a decision to be made. If we focus solely on the pain, we overlook the seeds of transformation that were planted by that pain. We miss the revelation that love can make pain beautiful, and a wound can become a path to awakening. If we let the light in, we can find the capacity to harness everything they gave us—the joy, the pain, the longing—and the free-will choice of what to do with all of it. In his song "Anthem," Leonard Cohen says, "There is a crack, a crack in everything. That's how the light gets in."

What if we all looked at our lives this way? Do you blame your past for your current hardships, or do you look for the opportunities in your challenges? How have your misfortunes changed you? Continuing with questions like these, you can begin to appreciate the bigger picture. What if you could learn to value the cracks?

A Larger Story

About a year after that routine but pivotal day, I published a book called *The Beautiful Disruption* about heartbreak, mental illness, and self-prophecy. When I wrote it, I had the intention of letting go of old stories so I could make room for new ones. I was doing it to let the light in, to find a healing narrative for painful memories. The process allowed me to revisit scenes from my life to see what wisdom they had to offer that I'd missed. To see what songs the words would make now that I'd found the language to write them. In this mix of truth and fiction, I created composite characters and scenes to maintain some privacy for those involved.

It was the first time I'd written so publicly about how my mother's condition affected me. The process made me realize the responsibility I have to the other characters in my story. I wrote the book to examine my life, not expose anyone. This is the role of nonfiction, particularly personal narrative, to share knowledge, wisdom, observations, and insights that reflect the human experience. In my storytelling workshops, I refer to this dynamic as *examination versus exposure.* As storytellers who are writing to heal, we must be clear on our motivation to ensure that we are coming from an ethical, constructive place. Examination is sharing your story to explore the complexity of human nature, the entanglements that everyday people find themselves in, and the impact we have on each other. Exposure is sharing your story for shock value or to seek revenge or attention without regard to how you portray others.

The characters are the heart and soul of any story. We—as tellers and consumers of stories—want to understand their fears, hopes, needs, desires, heartbreaks, and dreams. We want to see the characters grow and develop. We want to see ourselves and the people we know in the challenges they face. No one is all good or all bad. Each of us has a unique story that makes us who we are. Capturing the dimensionality of the characters in our stories is not only ethical but also acts in service of our healing, as it activates empathy and a broader perspective.

When I started writing down what I'd been afraid to say out loud, I found this broader perspective and a freedom I'd never felt before. The truth felt like a surge of power, a chance to forge a new path. I was no longer a victim or a villain; I was a character on a search for meaning, seeking a bigger, wider, more loving perception of myself and the world around me. The last line of the book summarizes the message I wanted to convey: "Love makes pain beautiful when a broken heart serves as the ultimate path to freedom." After I published *The Beautiful Disruption*, I kept writing to find more treasures within, and I never stopped.

We let the light in by accepting our inherent worthiness and seeing ourselves as the humans we are. Humans who want to be loved. Humans who have hurt and been hurt. Sharing my story was a way to practice bravery and approach my pain in a new way based on the idea that every experience has value. Instead of the world becoming unsteady when someone asked about my story, the meaning I found in writing it down gave me roots. Without meaning, I felt fragile, untethered. With a healing narrative, I was reinforced.

A Healing Narrative

Writing down our experiences not only helps us process what we've been through but also frees up cognitive resources, so we can imagine new possibilities for the future. To find a healing narrative and ease the burden of any old stories you're carrying, you can start by looking at specific events and separating the facts from your feelings. This is an approach that reveals the meaning of the experience in your life, so you can eventually release its power over you.

Creativity is a collaborative effort of the heart and mind. Research shows that when we integrate their wisdom, they work together to help the two hemispheres of our brains process our experiences cooperatively. In 1986, Dr. James Pennebaker, a social psychologist at the University of Texas at Austin, studied the impact that writing about traumatic experiences has on mental health. He and his colleagues found that when you write about disturbing life events by linking your feelings about the event to the facts, you can improve your overall well-being. Pennebaker developed a method called *expressive writing* that has specific guidelines: Write about a stressful, traumatic, or emotional experience in fifteen- to twenty-minute sessions that take place over a period of three to five days. In the first session, you write the facts. In the second session, you write your feelings about the facts. In the third session, you write the meaning you have assigned to the experience. For each session, you start the clock and write continuously without worrying about spelling or grammar. If you run out of things to write about, just repeat what you have already said. Since then, over two hundred research studies have reported that expressive or "emotional" writing can improve an individual's physical and emotional health. It can lower blood pressure; strengthen our immune systems; and reduce stress, anxiety, and depression.

Expressive writing leads you to a healing narrative by contextualizing your thoughts and beliefs. First, we must realize that our thoughts form our beliefs, which fuel our actions. Many of us think that our beliefs are facts, and there's nothing we can do to change them. By separating the objective facts from our feelings and thoughts, we discover there is room for interpretation. As you sit with the idea that your life can change when you change your thoughts, you realize this includes memories. Facts that you assumed were written in stone can be regarded with a new perspective.

Healing narratives not only explore the pain and distress but also acknowledge the contrasting joy, beauty, or simplicity present in the experience. The nurse who was so kind to you while you were in the hospital. The beautiful sunrise that greeted you the day after your loved one died. The moments and seasons of joy within a difficult childhood. Including the beauty doesn't negate the trauma, but it does awaken a wise witness consciousness inside that sees a more holistic representation of the experience. Even if you can't immediately recall any humor, beauty, or hope in the experience, you may be able to express observations of grace or kindness that sustained you. You may be able to describe the food that was cooking or the music that was playing, which adds a touch of levity and relief to the memory.

You now have the benefit of time, wisdom, and life lessons that put experiences in a new light. You can connect the dots and see the value in what you learned or the strength you found that you didn't know you had. Perhaps the experience gave you the knowledge to help someone else. Bringing your heart and mind together to find new meanings does *not* mean you are bypassing trauma or belittling what you went through. It doesn't change the objective facts. But it can help you reflect on your feelings *then* and your feelings *now*. It gives you the power to decide what meaning you are assigning to these facts and how they affect your present and future. This is how we bring creative thinking into our personal storytelling. Healing is when we are able to hold our stories with an open hand and look at them from different angles to find new meanings.

Reflecting and writing in this way not only helps you reimagine the experiences you've had; it creates a bigger vantage point to see beyond the patterns of your mind. Our thoughts are like pathways in our consciousness, and it can be difficult to think new thoughts and create new pathways if you're not in touch with your creativity. It's like choosing the path less traveled, the one that is obstructed by overgrowth and rocky terrain, the one we must pave with our courage and imagination. Our identities are so often entwined with the stories that play in our heads. We need to consider that these stories—especially our victim stories—can be changed. We have creative freedom. We can take a step back, imagine the story from a different point of view, and gain new insights. A healing narrative offers new ways to forgive, make peace, gain wisdom, and move on.

Reflection: What Else Could Be True?

> *Ultimately, then, writing about difficulties enables us to discover the wholeness of things, the connectedness of human experience. We understand that our greatest shocks do not separate us from humankind. Instead, through expressing ourselves, we establish our connection with others and the world.*
>
> —Louise DeSalvo

In chapter 1, I wrote about living the questions and discovering the limiting beliefs we have that are potentially holding us back. Some of the beliefs holding me back were that I was not a good person and that I was not strong enough to be there for my mother. In this current chapter, I am living my questions—grappling with my decision to stay distant from my mother, the grief of losing my father, and how their choices affected me. The visit to my friend's house illustrates how the belief that I was wrong for how I handled my mother's illness showed up as guilt and shame in my body anytime someone asked me about my parents. Eventually, I find a healing narrative by zooming out to look at the facts, my feelings then, my feelings now, and my hopes for the future.

Now it's your turn. For this exercise, keep in mind that you want to self-reflect gently without forcing anything that doesn't feel ready, and you want to have the support of a loved one or mental health professional as needed. This is a time for inner listening. Trust your feelings and body awareness to guide you. This is not a time to apply productivity goals or set strict expectations. It's more important to find a flow or rhythm that feels natural, inviting, and sustainable. Be gentle and self-nurturing through this process. Give yourself the kindness you would give to a younger version of yourself or someone you love going through a difficult time. Release self-criticism and judgment about yourself, your experience, and your creative expression. Release concerns about grammar, punctuation, and style. The intention is to find the simplest words you can to tell yourself that it's safe to face what happened and heal.

Choose an event or a circumstance from your past that captures how the limiting belief you wrote about in chapter 1 has shown up in your life. You're going to use aspects of the expressive writing method to write about it. For each step, set aside no more than twenty minutes to work on it at a time, no more than three times a week. Come back to it as many times as needed to complete the exercise.

- **Facts:** Choose an emotionally transformative event or moment in your life journey. Write down words, notes, phrases, sentences that come up when you think about the situation. Write as many factual and observational details as you can; nothing is too small to describe. What did you see, hear, taste, smell, touch during this experience?

- **Feelings:** Write about how this event emotionally affected you at the time. Explore your internal landscape. Link your feelings to the specific facts you described in the first part. What did you feel? Why did you feel this way? How did these feelings about this situation affect the bigger picture of your life? If you run out of things to say but you feel there is still more, look at a line you already wrote and ask yourself: What else is this connected to?

- **Healing:** Write about your perspective on this event now. Explore the things you know now that you didn't know before this event happened. How and when did your knowing change? What meaning do you assign to this experience? What lessons or discoveries did you take away from the experience? What universal truths do you recognize?

What do you learn about yourself from this exercise? I learned that another limiting belief that was alive in that moment at my friend's house was that my parents' silence would continue to be my silence. From the way my heart jumped in my chest, the ground swayed under my feet, and I lost my breath, I know that my body rejected that interpretation. Our bodies have a language all their own, don't they? We would do well to learn what our bodies are trying to tell us—how they communicate, how they warn us, how they guide us. For example, I know now that the rush of heat in my chest, the tightening in my gut, and the shaking of my hands are signs that my boundaries are being crossed in some way or that I am abandoning myself. Our bodies know our stories. How does your body speak to you when your limiting beliefs are activated or when your values are being ignored? In the next chapter, we will find more entry points to our stories and how our beliefs fuel our choices and perceptions.

Chapter Three

Fatal Flaw

Before I became a mom with three young kids who distanced herself from her mother, I was a teenager who thought that being a good girl who didn't cause problems would fix her family. From the day my mother accused me of flirting with my father, I began pretending and performing, trying to twist myself into a person she could find no fault with. This effort would shape my identity for years to come.

When you live with an unpredictable parent, you become keenly tuned in to their facial expressions, tone of voice, and body language. From day to night, I made decisions based on how I might be perceived by my mother, what might upset her, and what might pacify her. In the early '90s, the beginning of my adolescence, my bedroom was where I mastered the art of swallowing my feelings. I remember the bright mornings, waking up to a cheerful blur of silky robes and scarves in the shape of my mom. She would prance from room to room, opening windows and watering plants, with gospel music booming through the Magnavox stereo in my parents' room. One morning sticks out in my memory.

"What does my baby want for breakfast?" she sings as she breezes into my room smelling like Jean Nate body splash, playfully pulling the blanket off my long legs and grabbing my toes.

"Maybe scrambled eggs and toast?" I say carefully, rubbing the sleep out of my eyes so I can clearly see her reaction.

I answer her question based on what I think will keep her at ease. I would love some French toast, but scrambled eggs are a safer choice. In the words of poet Yrsa Daley-Ward in her poem "relief," I'd learned the art of folding my desire into itself to cater to my mother.

What was more important than my preference for French toast was the need to keep my mother in a good mood. What if we don't have any cinnamon? Or nutmeg? Her singsong voice might turn staccato. She might become agitated, her calm breeze turning into a tornado. She'd say that I chose French toast out of spite, knowing that we didn't have the ingredients for it, sending her on an ill-fated search just to torment her. I knew for sure that we had eggs and bread, and that was a choice that would keep the peace. I didn't answer based on what I wanted; I answered based on what I thought I could have without disturbing the fragile balance in our relationship. It was my duty to keep the peace by any means necessary. I altered myself in attempts to control the uncontrollable, but despite my efforts, there was always an unexpected reckoning waiting for me.

I remember the witching hours, waking up to my mother's demons in that same bedroom in the middle of the night. Many times, she sat on the cedar chest at the foot of my bed, a hunched-over shadow, partially lit by the streetlight shining through the curtained window. One such night, she sat in the same silky robe, the singsong greeting gone, leaving only the raspiness of her nighttime voice and the pounding of my heart in my ears. My mother never laid a hand on me, but when she had that remote look in her eyes, I was afraid of her. One day I would learn that it's common for schizophrenia symptoms to worsen at night.

"What were you doing in my closet? I can tell that you've been there. Did you hide something?" She directs her questions to the floor, the wall, her nails, her lap, looking everywhere but directly at me. My eyes look where she looks, hoping for a glimpse of what she sees.

Even though I have no idea what she's talking about, guilt forms a knot in my throat. She sees something bad and untrustworthy in me that I don't see. Tonight, like so many other nights, she is disappointed in me for things I didn't do or couldn't help. I want her to trust me. In my mind, the only choice is to play along, prioritize her reality and undermine my own—or risk losing her. It was easy to be silent when I knew that nothing I said would be believed.

As children, we naturally seek to please our parents to maintain a sense of safety. So I accepted what I thought was reality: We can't keep all of ourselves if we want to be loved. We must hide the parts that people—and specifically our loved ones—find unlovable. Crying only made things worse. Defending myself only fueled the fire. So I lay there, swallowed my misery, and waited for the episode to be over.

Looking back at your life, what did you learn to do to feel safe in your family? How much of your authentic self did you swallow in the effort to be loved? What did you hide to protect yourself? Who were you before your circumstances shaped who you thought you had to be?

Sacrifice Your Reality

Limiting beliefs take root in childhood when we innocently become attached to the roles and labels that adults assign to us. Words have the power to stick to us, particularly children, who don't have the life experience to question what they are told. We believe what adults tell us about who we are and who we should be.

I was praised for being well-mannered, doing well in school, and staying out of trouble. I was scolded for crying too easily, questioning my mother's accusations, and talking about family business outside of our home. I grew up wanting my mother to see the good in me, to believe that I was on her side and she was safe with me. But the dynamic we had was that "goodness" had to be proven; it wasn't assumed—in fact, it was always in doubt. She told me every day that she loved me, but she also accused me of plotting against her, which was disorienting, and I now wonder if that has anything to do with why I've had such a hard time trusting and believing in myself.

Growing up, I didn't see examples of how to feel my feelings and speak my truth in a healthy way. The women in my family taught me to be a good person, work hard, and love God. They didn't talk about their sadness and pain, and they didn't ask me about mine. My understanding was that everyone has problems and secrets, and it's not helpful to complain.

I faced the turbulence of my home life by piecing together an identity based on how I believed a Strong Black Woman should behave: We don't have the luxury of being emotional. We have to stay sharp and stretch ourselves to our limits to survive; that makes us strong. We don't talk about what hurts; that makes us weak. We don't whine about what we can't change; that makes us ungrateful. We take our worries to church. We leave them at the altar. We confess only to God.

According to Dr. Seanna Leath, assistant professor of community psychology at the University of Virginia, who researches issues related to the holistic development of Black girls and women, "The 'Strong Black Woman' stereotype is a cultural ideal and psychological coping mechanism. Black women are required to respond to life's hardships by portraying strength and concealing trauma."

In her study "How the Expectation of Strength Harms Black Girls and Women," she says, "My conversations with Black college women highlight that even as they were praised for taking care of siblings, helping around the house, and excelling academically, their emotional displays of vulnerability, anger, and sadness were often met with resistance from family members."

As a child prone to the emotionality that Dr. Leath mentioned, I expected to get tougher one day. I thought it was my birthright. To grow into the Strong Black Woman I was destined to be, I'd have to swallow my tears and build a tolerance for pain. Instead of crying when my mother accused me, I'd have to disconnect from my feelings and go somewhere else in my mind. Instead of trying to reason with her about what's real and what's not, I'd have to redirect my attention to other things: school, friends, boys, books. Escape was the only way I knew how to cope.

While I was cultivating these defense mechanisms, my sense of identity was breaking down. By ignoring the distress that was always lurking under the surface, I was slowly becoming a stranger to myself, but instead of fighting it, I welcomed it. I was grateful for this stranger who stood in for me when my mother's eyes went dark and I needed to hide.

I decided that this is how the world works. I must be who my family and friends need me to be, no matter what it costs me personally. I must honor family silences to protect the peace because open, honest discussion causes pain and drama. If people knew what was really going on in my household, something bad would happen. If people knew what was going on inside of *me*, something bad would happen. And this became what I expected from life: you sacrifice your reality to make others feel safe in theirs, and this secures your belonging.

This shows how a misunderstanding of facts, a decision from a wounded place, turned into a whole story that it is not safe to go against the grain, to rock the boat, to speak your truth.

This assumption, based on an unspoken familial agreement, was a low ceiling in my life that kept me from standing tall and holding my head up high. With this limited outlook, I wandered out of my confusing childhood into a womanhood of low self-worth and impending doom, from which it would take decades to escape.

What Remains Unspoken

Was it really even that bad? I've often asked myself this question. My parents did the best they could, and I never went unfed or unloved. For a long time, this kept me from acknowledging my sadness and resentment. *We don't have the luxury of being emotional. We don't talk about what hurts; that makes us weak. We don't whine about what we can't change; that makes us ungrateful.* But if anyone had asked, I would have told them about the part of me that was frozen in that moment when she first accused me, not just of doing something wrong but of being a bad person who wanted to hurt her. Why did I internalize that when I knew it wasn't true? Even decades later, it still burns. Why do our bodies hold on to wounds that we think our minds have already repaired?

Complex trauma is a psychological condition that comes from prolonged exposure to traumatic events that affect your sense of emotional or physical safety. It can arise in any circumstance where you experience fear, helplessness, or powerlessness over an extended period of time with the perceived or actual inability to escape. Even if you don't think of your childhood as traumatic, every human experience includes pain and heartache: war and terrorism, natural disasters and climate change, loss of friends and loved ones, illness and accidents, discrimination and injustice. These are all experiences that can be traumatic for children and adults alike, in addition to inherited pain from our parents, elders, and ancestors. Trauma comes in many different shapes and sizes.

You might be carrying painful memories of being bullied in school. You thought you got over it a long time ago, but you still lash out when you perceive that someone is teasing you. Maybe you grew up in a loving but financially insecure family, and you were always expecting the rug to be pulled out from under you. Now you are afraid to spend money, even on necessities. Perhaps you had a lot of energy and were routinely yelled at for being too busy, too loud, too active, which broke your spirit. Now you have a fear of expressing yourself. These small traumas are not acutely life-threatening, but they have mental, emotional, and physical impacts, negatively affecting your relationship with yourself and others.

The lack of open and honest acknowledgment of what hurts makes processing chronic emotional pain much more complex. The suppression of truth prevents help and solutions. You don't admit that you're suffering, maybe not even to yourself, so you don't ask for help. You don't ask, so you don't receive. This suppression can become a false premise on which you build the story of your life, leading to unwanted patterns. You wonder why you keep finding yourself in the same situations, the same dynamics in relationships, storylines that you've come to expect. You play your role—the victim, the troublemaker, the control freak, the angry one, the people pleaser, and so on—and perhaps you tell yourself that this is just who you are or how you have to be.

My need to prove that I was a good person affected every part of my life. No one could address any problem with me without me feeling unfairly attacked. If I wasn't someone's cup of tea, it was an indication of my worth. Our unhealed emotional wounds behave similarly to physical wounds. We may forget about them until we move or touch them the wrong way and feel a jolt of pain, leading to a knee-jerk reaction. We get used to changing the way we move our bodies to avoid that pain as much as possible. The childhood wound left by my mother's accusations did not start to heal until I admitted that underneath these reactions, I was in pain and needed help.

What stories have you told yourself to minimize unaddressed pain? How have the stories you've created hindered your ability to release that pain? What are the origins of these stories?

Family Values

Our families influence us: the joy, the pain, the gifts, the traditions—they're passed down through the generations. Families are full of flawed beings who give us habits, coping mechanisms, and tools for living, some by direction and some by example. We carry subtle imprints like how we laugh, the way we stand, how we eat, the jokes we tell. We carry personality traits like getting angry when we're scared, obsessing over what other people think, or avoiding difficult conversations. Sometimes we accept these birthrights without questioning them, even when they're painful.

I believe that a family, as an entity, has a soul. The family soul is a collective witness to the lives and times of the individual souls that are born through it. Through generations of births, marriages, migrations, and deaths, the family's identity evolves through the stories that are passed down, forged from the memories and imaginations of its members. Each family member has their version of events and their realities, as their stories blend to infuse the personalities of their offspring. Customs, rituals, and traditions are threads in this elaborate tapestry that have an infinite capacity to stretch and keep the individuals connected to the whole.

As we grow in age and observation, we become more aware of the patterns, beliefs, and expectations that form the myths of our families—first the openly acknowledged ones and eventually the hidden ones. At some point, we realize there are certain values and ways of being that we're holding on to from our families that don't necessarily align with who we are and how we want to live our own lives.

Can you think of roles and responsibilities you took on that required you to leave parts of yourself behind? Maybe in your family, you needed to be the jokester because somebody had to ease the tension. So you made jokes and pretended that nothing bothered you. Maybe you needed to be the strong one because no one was protecting you. Maybe you had to leave your need for nurturing behind. When you step into these roles, you may not be consciously aware that the adaptation is not who you are but rather a coping mechanism to survive in your environment.

Perhaps there are familial and cultural beliefs that you took on as your own that no longer resonate. Values and beliefs that you can look at squarely now and realize they don't reflect your worldview. Maybe you were taught that women don't get to be in charge or that men aren't allowed to cry. You may have been taught that people in your family never make a lot of money or that a religion you don't resonate with is the only path to God.

Many of us reach a point in our lives when the roles we've played and the identities we've forced ourselves into are smothering us. If you find yourself in conflict, unable to align with your family without betraying yourself, it can be a devastating realization that disrupts your life. Just as we have an instinct to protect ourselves, we have an instinct to protect and honor the soul of our families. Many of us think that if we don't cater to how things have always been, we are cutting the precious threads in the tapestry that hold the family together. But what if we're not cutting the threads? Instead, we are adding our unique stitch to the pattern.

We can understand the necessity for this evolution by recognizing that each generation has had to do different things to survive, and what our families pass on to us reflects their own expression of their experiences and stories. You can look at your family and reflect on the adversity that your parents faced and that their parents faced for some understanding of where their traditions, values, and coping mechanisms come from.

In her memoir *What My Bones Know*, Stephanie Foo confronts a history of abuse and explores how trauma can be inherited through generations. In an interview about the book, she says, "We are all products of our history. I don't really think it's surprising that we carry our fears, traumas, tics, and insecurities and pass them on to their children to some degree, whether it's a depression-era recipe for potato salad or a deep-seated fear of abandonment."

What did your family survive? What challenges and adversity did they face? What adventures and journeys did they take to find a better life or to expand their territory? What personality traits did these experiences cultivate? If you go beyond the surface of certain behaviors and traditions, you will find a pathway to origins that lend insight to what you want to carry forward and what you want to leave behind.

Maybe you've heard stories about your great-grandfather's stoic work ethic, never taking a day off, never showing a moment of vulnerability, which allowed him to protect and provide for his family and leave a legacy of strength. His survival skills have been passed down through the generations to your grandfather, to your father, to you. You carry on the hardworking legacy of your great-grandfather by being a force in your career and a rock for your family, but you also carry a fear of showing emotions, which proves challenging in your intimate relationships and sense of fulfillment.

A quality or belief that we inherited, which we might think is simply a part of our identity, could perhaps instead be an arrow pointing us in a new direction—to questioning, challenging, and finding a new way to move forward. One that goes against the way you've been taught to think and show up in the world. To reclaim your story, you may have to break spoken and unspoken agreements. Your duty is to speak and live and explore your truth, not to play a role to keep the peace or maintain the balance. No matter how disruptive the thought of this may seem, being your true self is what will create long-term healing and progress for you and the evolution of your family's soul. The discovered freedom here is that we can understand the way our predecessors persevered while also finding the courage to develop our own evolved ways.

From Tragedy to Rebirth

Believing that it was not safe to be myself became a rooted belief, a fatal flaw that led to a chain of thoughts and actions. Starting back in my childhood bedroom, I used to sit in silence, waiting for hallucinations and voices to emerge, almost inviting them, a twisted kind of solidarity with my mother. I was convinced there was no way to stop the descent. I lived my life with the assumption of this destiny for years. If she had to suffer in this way, then so would I. With a child's mind, I leaped to conclusions, and they became my facts. With no one to talk to, reframe things, or provide a different perspective, I spun a story of defeat. It was through writing and self-observation that I discovered my belief was empowering my fate.

My hopes for the future were limited by the beliefs I had about my mental stability. I did not think I could change what was coming to me. It was a matter of choice versus destiny, a theme that many of our favorite characters in books and movies have played out before us. A fate conflict occurs when a character is struggling with some kind of destiny, a predetermined fate or prophecy they must face. Similarly, the life choices we make because of our flawed beliefs can ultimately lead to our conceptual downfall—a life that never feels quite like a true reflection of who we are inside. We can see examples of this in literature when storytellers develop characters whose beliefs beckon events that lead to tragedy or comedy—or sometimes rebirth or transformation.

In his book *The Seven Basic Plots*, Christopher Booker breaks down the seven story plot types that he positions as the foundation of all storytelling: tragedy, rebirth, overcoming the monster, rags-to-riches, the quest, voyage and return, and comedy. We will break them down in the reflection at the end of the chapter, and you will recognize many, if not all, of them. They're not just tools for novelists and screenwriters. Anyone can use these frameworks to explore their personal stories and highlight plot points that give the details of their lives new meaning.

Let's first consider the tragedy story, which is when the main character is undone by a critical character flaw or the cruelty of fate. We will use this story plot as a starting point from which to reclaim our stories because most of us carry beliefs that there is something about us that we can't overcome. The tragic flaw may be a misjudgment or deficiency that leads to the character's downfall. Sometimes the protagonist gets it into their head that something in their life is missing—power, fame, a specific love interest, or something else—and they suffer trying to get it or due to the lack of it. The character's actions are fueled by their beliefs.

Our stories will seem destined for downfall when we define ourselves according to the worst events and circumstances that have happened to us. For so long, I told a sad story about my childhood and only referenced the most painful parts of my story as a prediction of what my future would be like. I only focused on the fatal flaw: the belief that I had to hide who I am, that my true self was inherently wrong and doomed. A belief that I carried with me into adulthood, that I fashioned into a story of why I was destined to struggle.

Then I had kids, and as they grew, I started seeing life through their innocent eyes. How could I model a different story for them, something—anything—other than accepting defeat? They made me think about how I could transform my doomed destiny into a journey of resilience instead of a tragedy story that I unknowingly passed down to them. Wisdom can be inherited through generations too. I realized that I'd have to forgive myself for what I didn't know and the assumptions that I made when I was younger. I could look at my journey as what needed to happen to awaken me so I could contribute to the generational wisdom and add my unique stitch to the tapestry.

Story work has given me the perspective to model honesty and compassion when I talk about my family of origin and our challenges. I want my kids to feel connected to the soul of our family and recognize that they have their part of the story as well. The journey of life teaches you to value your challenges and find your way by learning from them. How you grow from the peaks and valleys contributes courage, authenticity, and resilience to the family line.

Since this shift in perspective, I've been intrigued by the exploration of choice versus destiny and the opportunity to explore what we have control over and what we don't in our lives. Perhaps within that exploration, we can find the truest blend of our evolutionary instincts and the active choices we make from experience and earned wisdom.

Plotting a New Story

What matters most is not the events of our lives but the storylines we create from them. By staying in the small room of my silence, self-doubt, and self-denial, I created a narrow storyline of doom and defeat, a tragedy story. Using Christopher Booker's seven story plots, I can arrange events into an arc and explore different interpretations to find hope and possibility. For example, if I were telling a rebirth story instead of a tragedy story, what experiences would I highlight, and how might this character arc change my self-concept and my outlook on the future?

Remember, the main character in a tragedy has a doomed outcome due to some kind of fatal flaw or misconception. This story could be about a villain (or misguided innocent) who goes down a dark road that ends in destruction—either a literal or symbolic death or loss. The main character in a rebirth has been under a negative or limiting influence, and during the course of the story, they encounter a person or situation that inspires them to see the world differently and break free.

My tragedy story is about a girl with no voice or backbone, who believes she is destined to become mentally ill like her mother and unable to live a quality life. She uses this belief to play the role of a victim and not show up as her true self, which leads to years of struggle. Motherhood provides a portal for rebirth and clarity, and the desire to end generational cycles inspires her to see the world differently and release these old beliefs.

Here are some other ways I could reshape my story to find meaning through the basic plots:

You are likely familiar with overcoming the monster. In this story, the main character (you) must dig deep for the strength to overcome a monster or an evil of some sort that is seemingly larger, greater, or smarter than you. The monster could be a physical one or a conceptual one. In my version of this, family secrets that are beyond my understanding threaten to silence my voice, but through books, art, and friendship, I find superpowers that allow me to conquer the "silence" monster that held my truth captive and stifled my ability to live a fully expressed life.

The main character in a rags-to-riches story grows up in poor living conditions and must go through obstacles to find their way to wealth and prosperity. There are often ups and downs in which the character achieves some success and then loses it because they still have a lesson to learn. In my version of this, I grew up metaphorically poor in truth telling, and

I experience peaks and valleys as I learn in many hard but rewarding ways the value of emotional honesty and gradually become rich through the power of my voice.

The next two story archetypes are the quest and the voyage and return. In both, the main character sets out on a physical or spiritual mission to find a person, place, or thing that requires them to face tests and obstacles. The voyage-and-return story takes the quest further because the main character is unexpectedly transported to a whole different world or universe with mysteries that must be solved before they can escape and return home. In my version of this, I go on a quest away from my family to find my own values and meaning. I discover new worlds like college, corporate America, and creative entrepreneurship, which introduce me to new lands and different cultures. Finally, I come home and must figure out how to exist with the same family while keeping my values.

In a comedy story, the main character is drawn to a certain person or situation, maybe a job or ideal, but there is an obstacle in the way, and it's presented with humor or chaos. Eventually, the confusion is cleared up, and the main character learns something about themselves and lives happily ever after, with some version of their goal being actualized. In my version of this, I would use dark humor to tell you about my trauma and how it showed up in adulthood through ill-advised decisions about money and men.

Through these newly formed pathways, the events of our lives don't change, but we change the meaning we assign to our life experiences, so they expand us instead of limiting us.

Grieving Your Old Story

I didn't wake up to my own tragic self-prophecy until I went to therapy and started writing about my life. I learned how to use writing, not just to vent but to see myself, to see the way I was thinking and the meaning I was making. I saw that I was so identified with this tragic identity that I didn't know who I was without it. Part of me liked the pity and the drama. It made me feel generous to carry this weight on my back. Every challenge that life gave me was an excuse to blame my circumstances and stay stuck. While I felt the weight of my limiting beliefs, deep down I didn't want to leave the island of misfit toys, where I could stay broken.

There's a saying that people are more likely to choose a familiar pain over an unfamiliar joy. Familiar pain feels like home. Unfamiliar joy doesn't feel like joy at all at first; it feels like a sort of death. There's a grieving that takes place because we think these roles we've played and these stories we've fed into have protected us, for better or worse, when we were our most vulnerable, as innocents. So of course it's hard to let them go. We want to keep them, and letting go feels like a dislocation, like a part of your identity is dying.

The thought of this is scary when you don't know who you'll be without the familiar pain. You find the motivation to move through the discomfort by realizing that it's your calling and responsibility to create your own part of the tapestry, to stitch your part of the story. We have to remember that honoring our roots doesn't mean we need to resist our evolution. Humans are wired to evolve and innovate, so much so that if we don't, we can hurt our chances of survival. The family's soul knows this and plants a unique calling in each child, knowing there are different ways the light can get in.

We all know how it feels to look back at difficult events from the past and wish we could change them. But this wish only leaves us feeling stuck in an unquenchable desire to control the uncontrollable. When I started looking back at my life as a silent witness instead of a victim, my perspective changed. I saw the role I played differently. Hindsight, whether you go back ten years ago or ten days ago, can offer new insights if you choose to look without bias. Guilt, regret, blame, scarcity, and shame are just a few reasons we miss out on these new insights because they serve as blinders keeping us from discovering the truths they hide.

We can't control what happens to us, but we have the choice to be empowered or disempowered by our experiences. Did the abuse you experienced make you cold, or did it deepen your capacity to be kind and compassionate toward others? Do you blame your past for your current circumstances, or do you look for opportunities in your challenges?

Using the seven story frameworks to work with our stories, we can take stock of the plot points that make up the story, the highs and lows, the joy and pain. This examination makes you acknowledge how you overcame, what was at stake, and what choices you made and why. Instead of your struggles being the defining factors of your story, this exercise will highlight the life lessons and values that are the building blocks of a new, empowered story.

Reflection: New Storylines

> *The past created the present but the present also recreated the past.*
>
> —NADJA SPIEGELMAN

When you start believing and telling better stories about yourself, you have the power to change the path ahead. Your life will become more vibrant, more purposeful, more inspired. When you don't find an empowering way to interpret your life, you become more susceptible to the world's interpretations. The following exercise shows you how to take back your power and use creative thinking to apply a new storyline to an old story. First, let's review.

In chapter 1, I asked you to reflect on a limiting belief that is affecting your life and ask yourself some burning questions about what else could be true. In chapter 2, I asked you to choose an event or circumstance from your past that captures how the limiting belief you wrote about in chapter 1 has shown up in your life so you can recognize the life lessons that came from the experience. These are all tools to help you approach your life story with fresh eyes, so the past doesn't just create the present, but you also have the power to re-create the past. In chapter 3, we are referencing the seven basic plots to use our imaginations to find new perspectives.

Many of us are playing the protagonist in our own tragedy stories because we have a misconception or circumstance that we think will ultimately lead to our downfall in some way or, at best, will prevent us from living the lives we really want. Referencing the seven basic plots, we can use our imaginations to find new perspectives. Your so-called fatal flaw is just one plot point of many. Being intentional about the plot points you choose to highlight, you can rewrite any tragedy story you might be carrying to center the values and life lessons that allow you to thrive despite the difficult circumstances—or fatal flaws—in your life.

You might be thinking, *My life hasn't been a tragedy at all!* Perhaps the word *tragedy* sounds a bit intense, but for the context of this exercise, remember we are looking at the word *tragedy* as a story plot for creative purposes. You are going to focus on a misconception (fatal flaw) that has created a disempowering storyline (tragedy) that has wreaked havoc on your self-concept and life trajectory, and you're going to transform the story from a tragedy into any of the other six plots to find a creative vision for your life that inspires you.

While you do this exercise, think about the experiences and influences that created the misconception (fatal flaw), and then also think about the experiences and influences that triggered a change of heart, mindset, and behavior. Notice where struggle revealed opportunity. Reflect on the moments of choice, challenge, and change and which factors and motivations fueled your decisions.

- What is your tragedy story (or defeated storyline)?
- Use your imagination to transform your tragedy story into one or more of the following:
  → **Rebirth**—The main character in a **rebirth** story has been under some kind of negative or limiting influence, and during the course of the story, they encounter a person or situation that inspires them to see the world differently and break free.

  Write about a person or situation in your life that has inspired you to see the world differently. Be specific about what you learned from this person or situation and how your perspective changed.

  → **Overcoming the Monster**—In this story, the main character (you) must dig deep for the strength to overcome a monster or evil of some sort that is seemingly larger, greater, or smarter than you. The monster could be a physical one or a conceptual one.

  What is the monster (physical or conceptual) that you have been struggling with? What special but perhaps overlooked or undervalued gifts do you have that can help you overcome this monster?

  → **Rags to Riches**—The main character in a **rags-to-riches** story grows up in poor living conditions and has to go through obstacles to find their way to wealth and prosperity. There are often ups and downs along the way, through which the character achieves some success and then loses it because they still have a lesson to learn.

  Identify an area of your life where you have experienced ups and downs, feast and famine. What obstacles have you faced? In what ways have you overcome those obstacles? What have you had to learn, or what do you think life is calling you to learn, through this dynamic?

→ **The Quest**—The main character sets out on a physical or spiritual mission to find a person, place, or thing that requires them to face tests and obstacles.

What have you gone on adventures to find? What were you seeking, and what did you have to overcome to find it? What was your motivation?

→ **Voyage and Return**—The voyage-and-return story takes the quest further because the main character is unexpectedly transported to a whole different world or universe with mysteries that must be solved before they can escape and return home.

Where have your adventures taken you beyond the boundaries of your familiar environment? What have been your rabbit holes and yellow brick roads that have led you to otherworldly adventures? What challenges did you face on this journey?

→ **Comedy**—The main character is drawn to a certain person or situation, maybe a job or ideal, but there is an obstacle in the way, and it's presented in an amusing or chaotic way. Eventually the confusion is cleared up, and the main character learns something about themselves.

What person, place, or thing have you been drawn to and faced obstacles to pursue? Reflect on it and highlight the moments of levity and comedy that shine through in the midst of the challenges, punctuating the struggle with lightness and humor.

Part II

Truths and Lies

Wounding and healing are not opposites. They're part of the same thing. It is our wounds that enable us to be compassionate with the wounds of others. It is our limitations that make us kind to the limitations of other people. It is our loneliness that helps us to find other people or to even know they're alone with an illness. I think I have served people perfectly with parts of myself I used to be ashamed of.

—Rachel Naomi Remen

Chapter Four

Masks We Wear

When I lean in to hug my friend's husband on their wedding day in 2006, my MAC bronzer leaves a trail of reddish-brown powder on the shoulder of his white tux. Embarrassed, I continue down the reception line like nothing happened. The August sun is beaming down on my face as my sweat turns the layers of bronzer I desperately applied that morning into a melted mess. I'd forgotten my usual foundation when I packed for the trip from Baltimore to Pittsburgh, and all I had with me was this loose bronzer powder. I knew the direct sunlight would be unforgiving, so I piled it on even though you're supposed to apply it sparingly to create a glow, not for coverage. In my mind, it was better to have some camouflage than none at all. I was twenty-nine years old, and revealing my naked face in the light of day was just as terrifying as baring my whole body.

I'm flanked by two of my closest friends that day, and I sandwich myself between them to hide as we walk into the reception. As soon as we find our seats, I escape to the bathroom to assess the damage. I wipe off the sweat and remaining makeup with brown paper towels from the dispenser and resign myself to the fact that I will have to go without my usual mask for the rest of the reception.

I spend the evening at the table avoiding up-close conversation and trying to cover the blemishes on my cheeks and jaw with my hair. Not even "Before I Let Go" or "Let's Stay Together," quintessential Black wedding songs, could get me out of my seat and into the mood of the occasion. Over seventeen years later, I look back on that day and shudder with regret. I remember little about the wedding outside of my loop of distorted, nervous thoughts about how disheveled I looked and how messy my life was. I was still fighting with the belief that something about me was hopelessly wrong and unacceptable in some way. It didn't matter where I was; these self-pitying moods could hit and pull me in like quicksand.

On that humid wedding day in my twenty-ninth year, my tragedy storyline was in full effect, and I was just beginning to notice it. I let my insecurities distract me from enjoying a major milestone in my friend's life that day. I look back and see myself sitting at the table, uncomfortable in my skin, lost in my drama. I want to tell that version of myself that she is not distraught because of the blemishes on her skin but because of her belief that those blemishes make her unworthy to take up space. I want her to know that hiding behind a mask, conceptually and physically, is preventing her from honoring her desire for true presence and connection.

Makeup was just one of the masks I wore to feel safe. Not everyone who wears a lot of makeup is hiding insecurities, but that's what *I* was doing, and I wasn't very good at it. The layers formed an outer shell to distract the world from seeing how broken I was inside. My hair was another wall of protection. When I was a little girl, I discovered that I could get attention with my hair. I was never the coolest or the smartest, but my hair was always a distinguishing characteristic. I learned how to braid it, twist it, and roll it up in a dozen different ways. I learned how to cover the acne on my cheeks with it. Even as I went through adolescent awkwardness, my hair always made me feel a little more secure.

I figured that if people approved of the appearances I created, then they wouldn't see that underneath the hair and makeup, I'm not likable enough, smart enough, holy enough, tough enough. If anyone looked too closely, the illusion would melt away just like the MAC bronzer, and I'd be exposed.

Masks can be both physical and emotional. We put them on and take them off to keep us safe from harm, to reveal and repress our secrets. They can serve as a place to hide, and they can also be a source of expression. Cultures all over the world use physical masks as part of rituals and traditions and to express individual and group identity. Imagine what we can learn about ourselves and our life stories by studying the physical, emotional, and metaphorical masks we wear. In this chapter, we are going to focus on the masks we wear as defense mechanisms, how they alter our stories, and the wisdom we can find by exploring the reasons we wear them. With these observations, we can make conscious decisions about the masks that allow for fuller expression and the ones that don't allow us to shine.

Stories behind the Masks

In the first three chapters, we reflected on our roots and origins, separating what is ours and what is not when it comes to the pain, trauma, beliefs, values, and myths that have orchestrated our lives. I hope you are experiencing new insights and impulses as letting go of limiting beliefs frees up your mind to explore new ideas and develop new thought patterns. These new insights and impulses lead us to take inspired action steps that align with our values and visions instead of our doubts and fears. Whether that's happening for you yet or not, stay the course and trust the process. Letting go of limiting beliefs and habits is not easy or quick. Story work is about slowly building a long-term creative approach to living, made up of daily choices. Later in our journey, we will get into practical ways to shape our daily choices with supportive thoughts and habits.

To discover the stories behind the masks we wear, we start by recognizing false identities that keep us from harnessing the power of our true selves. As we move through life, we adopt these false identities to conform to our environments, and we may not be aware of where our authenticity stops and the adaptations begin. Acknowledging the different faces we wear is uncomfortable, but it comes with the promise that removing our masks will unleash something powerful: the courage to face the world without hiding. Our masks prevent us from seeing the possibilities available to us as our true selves.

Masks can take on many shapes and forms. We mask with our facial expressions when we wear smiles to hide our sadness. Sometimes we mask with our defense mechanisms when we lash out in anger to hide fear and anxiety. We mask with our titles and roles when we don't know who we are without them. Masking can show up as saying things you don't mean in order to feel safe or making jokes when you're uncomfortable. These are all masks hiding something that makes us feel vulnerable, and often we don't even know what we're hiding because the reasons are buried so deeply in our subconscious mind.

You might think your masks are protecting you, but they are blocking you from finding a more empowered storyline for your life. While masks can serve as a form of self-preservation in some cases, they also lead to anxiety, stress, and loss of identity. When I was working in corporate America, I wanted so badly to be more assertive and confident, but there was no way to *truly* embody those qualities when I was so afraid of being discovered as a fraud. Whispers of unworthiness pervaded my inner thoughts. The sadness that underpinned my life at the time was empowered by the pain I'd never dealt with, which was always in contrast with the happy, easygoing image I presented on the outside. Eventually, this inner conflict caused so much disruption that I couldn't ignore it. The fear of exposure became less than the fear of staying at odds with myself.

To study our masks and find the courage to take them off, we must open new pathways in our minds, starting with asking ourselves heart-opening questions: If it wasn't safe in your family to show your emotions, what masks did you develop to hide them? If you were punished for being too loud and boisterous, what masks did you adopt to gain acceptance and love? If your environment growing up was unpredictable and chaotic, what masks did you develop to exert some control in your life? If your culture was unaccepting of your lifestyle choices, what masks did you put on to conceal yourself?

These questions may trigger small earthquakes that shake your foundation and leave you unsteady, so be gentle with yourself and remember that the masks we wear come from our instinct to protect ourselves and survive. It's not easy to let go of what once made you feel safe. We can get stuck there between our old narratives and the new ones we want to create. Whether it's a physical mask or an emotional one, before we can think about how to take off these barriers of protection, let's explore a philosophy for identifying the masks we wear and the impact they have on our life choices.

Three Faces

There is a Japanese philosophy that says everyone has three faces. The first face you show to the world. This is the public image that you present at work, in social environments, perhaps when you first meet someone. There are both true and false aspects to this display. You may hide parts of yourself to fit in with your environment. The first face has variations that depend on the situation, and the goal is to avoid being judged and cast out from a group from which you crave acceptance.

For example, one version of my first face was corporate Gina. She invested in physical masks: makeup, hair, clothes, shoes. Again, there's nothing objectively wrong with these things.

But in my case, I was using them to seek approval and hide my sense of lack. I spent beyond what I could afford to keep up the appearance of success. I based a great deal of my self-worth on how I looked, believing that I was hopelessly flawed on the inside so I had to be flawless on the outside. My financial life suffered the most from these misguided beliefs because my decision-making compass was so off course and out of sync with my truth and my values. Overspending was a conceptual mask that concealed how deluded I was about how to feel worthy and find fulfillment. When I felt ugly, I bought. When I felt sad, I bought. When I was bored, I bought. When I was happy, I bought. Like a drug, spending money put me under a spell that made me feel free but only for fleeting moments, and it was always followed by regret and withdrawal. For me, the financial and emotional cost of this first face was more than I could afford, and it was only a matter of time before I could no longer maintain it. And that's one of the questions you can ask yourself: What are the characteristics of my first face, and how much is it costing me to keep it up?

The second face you show to your close friends and family. Usually, they get a truer version of us than we give the rest of the world with the first face, but there are still conditions, especially depending on the nature of those relationships. This face changes as we transform from child to adult. We might have different parts of ourselves that come out to play with different friend groups. We might have layers of ourselves we hide from family members to avoid their disapproval. What we feel safe to reveal in one relationship may be different than in another.

It's wise to be discerning about what you reveal or don't reveal in your relationships. You don't have to tell your religious grandmother specifics about last weekend's wild one-night stand (unless she's cool like that). There's no need to share your darkest secret with a friend who is known for their lack of discretion. There's nothing wrong with trusting your intuition about what to share with whom. The problem is when your side of the relationship is altered by fear of judgment, criticism, or rejection, and you have to abandon yourself to maintain the relationship.

Due to my history with my mom, I was always concerned about being perceived as a good-intentioned person, and I wanted the people close to me to feel emotionally safe in our interactions. Sometimes this took the shape of mimicking the dominant behavior, even if it made me uncomfortable. Or going to dinner with friends because it was someone's birthday, even if I couldn't afford the choice of restaurant. Or having a family gathering at my place and preparing for it by purchasing a haul of new decor to make my home look more put together. I was more concerned about avoiding judgment and conflict than being true to myself.

The third face is the truest reflection of who you are. You may never show this face to anyone, and you may even be scared to acknowledge it yourself. This is you without the pain and shame you've experienced in life and without the external influence of the world. Many of us forget this part of ourselves because we've hidden our vulnerabilities so well for so long. Some of us never get to know the third face because we fear what we'll discover when we investigate.

It may be a shock when you realize that you are reshaping yourself to manage other people's perceptions of you, and sometimes it takes a rock-bottom moment to fully acknowledge how this effort is creating unnecessary friction in your life. In the aftermath of my friend's wedding, I started romanticizing what it would be like to experience life in a more authentic way, but I didn't know how to turn awareness into action.

The parts of ourselves that we most want to hide hold the key to our healing, evolution, and creative expansion. If our masks hide the truths that we think the world will not accept, then by studying them, we can discover what we need to accept within ourselves.

What will you find when you take off your masks? In what ways do masks allow you to hide or express parts of yourself that you fear won't be accepted? Questions like these are great places to look for narratives and stories that are at play in your life. Whatever you think you need to hide has power over you; diminishes your authentic needs, desires, and expressions; and keeps you from moving on to a new storyline. So how do we take back that power? Where do we start? How do we reconnect with our native intuition, remembering who we were before we started altering ourselves, before shame got in the way? We can rediscover this face by reconnecting with our innate creativity and remembering who we were before the world told us who to be.

Creativity Cultivates Authenticity

As children, we are effortlessly creative and emotionally honest. Eventually, that uninhibited, wholehearted expression begins to feel unsafe. We are teased, punished, or ostracized when we don't tone down our differences and quirks. That is when we are introduced to the discomfort of inauthenticity, the gap between how we show up in the world and who we really are. Self-awareness comes when we make connections between these self-departures and their deeper origins, when waves of memory, emotion, and imagination begin to show us patterns.

Let's go on a journey back to childhood, specifically to observe when we started developing different faces, when our third face became more distant and the first and second faces emerged. We can look at highs and lows in our lives to recognize when we were most in tune with ourselves, when we were not, and what was going on. This reflection will help us remember who we are when we are unmasked and why it's worth the effort to consider what that self-possession could look like now. I will recall moments when I was uninhibited by pain and insecurity, as well as the consequences of not being true to myself. I will show you how revisiting the creative outlets of my youth served as a passageway out of denial and avoidance back to my inner child and imagination, where I could reconnect with the pure expressive energy that once filled me with joy and wonder.

Highs and Lows

When I go back to moments in childhood when I felt most alive and inspired, the first place I think of is church. Wide-eyed, I sat every Sunday morning, waiting for the songs to surround me. Cotton-candy hair in two ponytail puffs held together by bright-colored ballies. Baby-oiled brown skin. I took deep breaths to stay calm while the choir sang. Gospel music created electricity in my veins that made me want to dance up and down the aisle one minute and fall out bawling on the pew the next. The Holy Ghost moved through the sanctuary on currents of harmonized sound, making people raise their hands in the air and jump out of their seats.

It was the mid-1980s, and when we got to Mt. Ararat Baptist Church early enough, my mother and I sat on the first floor, close enough to see the sweat on the choir director's brow. I loved to feel the beat of the drum pounding through my chest, hypnotized by the sounds of praise, a roller coaster racing inside.

I remember this high. I've been chasing it ever since. I felt it in church through the vibrations of the choir. I felt it when I was having a deep conversation with a friend or family member. I felt it from the actors when I went to the theater, and I felt it from my fellow dancers when we leaped across the stage in recitals. I felt it when I visited new places and when I smiled at strangers who smiled back. My mother told me this feeling came from God, and I'm thankful that she did because I latched on to that truth, and it became my anchor as I rode the waves of growing up, including the rough waters of her mysterious mental illness.

I escaped the tension in my childhood home by creating characters, making up dances, and acting out dramatic scenes from books and musicals. *The Wiz. Annie. Fame. The Five Heartbeats.* Movies saved back to back on VHS tapes with squiggly static lines at the bottom of the screen. Creative play and daydreaming made it possible to access that warm God energy at any time. In elementary school, I took ballet, tap, and jazz and sang in the chorus, and I found the high there too. Music and dance moved emotions through my body and allowed me to show my true self without fear of being misunderstood or having my words twisted, which often happened at home. In these moments, there was no disconnection between me and my higher self, no mask between my real face and the world.

When I got older, I was introduced to the shortcuts that life has to offer. Instead of getting my highs naturally, I reached for shortcuts like romance, sex, drugs, alcohol, food, money, achievement. Many costly decisions that I would come to make in my early adult years were attempts to make things happen in my time and in my way because I didn't trust life to provide the outcomes I wanted. By that time, the tragedy storyline had taken hold, and I believed that I needed to hide my wonder and innocence behind a more worldly, polished image. Scarcity took the place of creativity. Low took the place of high.

I remember taking deep breaths while I waited for the sheriff to come evict us. It's 2002, and I'm sitting in the living room of our Baltimore apartment looking around, imagining the knock on the door, the strangers invading our home, the neighbors watching. Soon our treasures would be piled up and thrown out on the curb like trash—the picture frames outlining our smiling faces, the pots and pans our parents had donated for our first home, the furniture my roommate and I put our entry-level money together to buy. Each second was a minute, each minute an hour while I sat there expecting a squad car to pull up at any moment. When my friend showed up with the certified check in time and we didn't get evicted, my relief only went skin deep. There was relief that I wouldn't have to tell my family. There was relief that I wouldn't have to deal with the embarrassment. Relief that I would not be revealed as an impostor who wasn't as put together as I presented myself to be.

I remember this low. I'd been clinging to it for too long. I have not gone a day in my life without clean water, food, or shelter, but I always expected life to be a struggle. There was something I was missing. Was it street smarts? Common sense? A certain edge? A backbone? I wasn't sure, but I didn't want anyone else to notice. Adulthood was like being a kid at the grown-up table—many of the conversations went over my head, but I wanted to belong there. I had no idea what I was doing, after all, so I surrounded myself with people I admired and did what I saw them doing. With that strategy, I walked on shaky ground and worried constantly that someone would notice how out of place and confused I was.

I quietly filed for bankruptcy when I was twenty-three years old, a year into my first job after college and pregnant with my first child. I'd accumulated thousands of dollars of debt in my five years as an adult, and I was desperate for a clean slate before my son arrived. I put on the mask of an educated, gainfully employed single mom. Underneath, I hid the emotionally unstable girl who was flaky with money and unable to set boundaries. Never mind facing reality, I put my energy into protecting the illusion, keeping my clusters of chaos hidden and unexamined.

I added bankruptcy to a running list of failures that included getting kicked out of the honors program in college, graduating late, and getting pregnant before I knew how to take care of myself. Each failure was a tiny death, my good-girl mask fading with each disappointment. I had a promising job at a prestigious financial services firm, where I made more than enough money to pay my half of the $550 rent, but I was being evicted for no other reason than lack of life skills and self-control. What if my coworkers found out? If I wasn't the high achiever that people expected me to be, then who was I? If I wasn't seen as smart, responsible, and upwardly mobile, then how would I be perceived?

Far from the recitals and performances of my youth, I developed a new kind of song and dance, a new kind of pretending and performing. If I wished I was fine when you asked me, I pretended to be. If I wanted to paint a pretty picture of my messy life, I altered the details, beautified the clutter, and presented the ideal. This habit lived on from childhood, when I hid what was wrong at home to keep up appearances in public.

Wearing masks kept my imaginary world in place. Corporate Gina allowed me to escape my reality. The character was based on what I thought were the most likable aspects of the real me: calm and kind, well adjusted, success oriented. The character hid what I thought were the most unlikable aspects of the real me: overly sensitive, socially awkward, incompetent. I saw the character as more of a protection than a lie, but hiding my true self became increasingly heavy and unsustainable.

The Pain of Hiding

Before we go any further, let's define authenticity: the quality of being real or true. Our authenticity is our power. In *The Seat of the Soul*, author Gary Zukav says that external power comes from outside sources like status, wealth, and possessions. Authentic power, however, has its roots in the deepest source of our being and involves aligning the personality with the soul:

"Our deeper understanding leads us to another kind of power, a power that loves life in every form that it appears, a power that does not judge what it encounters, a power that perceives meaningfulness and purpose in the smallest details upon the Earth. This is authentic power. When we align our thoughts, emotions, and actions with the highest part of ourselves, we are filled with enthusiasm, purpose, and meaning. Life is rich and full." When we are in touch with our authentic power, we are not making life choices based on external demands and expectations; we are aligning with our values without attachment to outcomes, knowing that we have the most creative control when we act from this place.

When we deny who we authentically are, we injure ourselves; we invite stress and weaken our connection to our inner guidance. The disconnection from my authentic self was painful, but it was a familiar pain. Hiding who you really are, in whatever form that takes, puts you in a sort of prison—a prison of secrets because there is always a fear of being found out. When we're living this way, we are not aware that the truth we are so afraid of is the pathway to healing. Under the mask is our true beauty, but we don't know that because society gives us different messages. Social cues teach us that we aren't supposed to be vulnerable and imperfect in public. We are supposed to measure up to an external standard. We think we are supposed to position ourselves to be accepted, even if we have to betray our true selves to do it.

One could certainly argue that too much authenticity is just as harmful as too little. Reflect on someone you have known in your life (perhaps you, if it applies) whose authenticity has held them back. Perhaps they hold rigidly to one version of themselves instead of allowing themselves to evolve and change. Perhaps their authenticity leads them to overshare without discretion, which jeopardizes their relationships. Willful authenticity can give the perception of self-absorption, excessive emotionality, or lack of boundaries. There is a difference between being genuine and open, and dumping your private matters onto others. Researcher and author Brené Brown says, "Vulnerability minus boundaries is not vulnerability." She suggests that before you decide to reveal a hidden part of yourself, ask, "Are you sharing your emotions and your experiences to move your work, connection, or relationship forward? Or are you working your s--t out with somebody?" Being mindful of your motivation is key.

The pain of hiding should not be replaced with a lack of discretion. Finding the balance is a personal experiment that requires practice. It would not have been helpful to walk into work the day after my almost eviction and say, "Hey everyone, I almost got evicted yesterday!" But it would have been helpful to reach out to someone I trust who could help me take steps to better manage my finances. Asking for help was not in my wheelhouse because it meant taking off my mask. It's hard to solve problems and find a new direction when you're still in the same mindset that created the problem. There is a mindset shift that is needed, which allows you to unmask and gain access to solutions.

Authenticity, just like any other virtue, requires discernment, and we learn that by doing the inner work to get back in touch with what matters to us and the impact we want to have in the world. Once we do that, we can practice the adjustments that come with aligning our actions with those values. This is where we learn that authenticity is an art, one that we practice so that we can remain in integrity with ourselves while still being mindful of our boundaries and motivations.

Experiment with Unmasking

From growing up in confusion, to the worldly discoveries of college, to the journey of working motherhood, I knew I wasn't the only one performing, but that only increased my justification of playing along. Playing along can land us in a life that may make sense and look good to other people but feels unfulfilling to us.

My writing career has been my own experiment in unmasking. I used to sit in meetings at work and daydream about a life where I wore my truth on my sleeve, writing books and sharing my story to help others feel less alone. In my vision, my blazers and slacks were replaced by harem pants and knitted sweaters; my cubicle was replaced by a cozy home office. When I took a leap of faith and started to pursue my writing professionally, I created a pen name so I could keep my creative writing separate from my corporate identity. I wrote at lunchtime, late at night after putting the kids to bed, in parking lots while chauffeuring them around. Awakened, I couldn't stop if I wanted to.

In 2009, I started a blog with one of my best friends where we wrote about our self-discovery journeys, womanhood, motherhood, spirituality, all of the things we were experiencing. I wrote without filter—notes, confessions, poems, essays, declarations. My diary on display. My becoming on display. I felt more comfortable sharing this side of me with strangers than people in my personal life who might judge me or not take me seriously, or be uncomfortable with my vulnerability. These consequences felt fatal to me at the time. Corporate Gina was afraid to take up space, so I created GG Renee, and she was not afraid. She was inspired and hopeful, and I trusted her.

I knew I was on the right track because I recognized the high I felt when I was working with stories, and writers, and words. I let my creative urges guide me. I joined the chorus of Black women writing about their transition from relaxed to natural hair. I saw my reflection in the other women who were sharing their stories and, in their own way, doing a version of unmasking, letting their natural texture grow out so they could fall in love with this hidden, and often criticized, part of themselves. There was a collective energy at the time that we all felt, and it fueled a creative revolution that I was thrilled to be part of. I was also surprised because I never imagined this is what my plot twist would look like. Creative expression brought me back to my true nature.

When I felt that high in church, I was valuing the joy of creative expression, kindness, and the honest sharing of love between people. When I was experiencing the low of almost getting evicted, I was suffering from the lack of values like being wise, responsible, and trustworthy. It hurt on a soul level to value these things and still to have my actions defy them, being out of integrity with myself and, on top of that, all the effort it took to hide it and pretend the image matched the reality.

From my lows, I learned that I want to be liked and accomplished and was willing to pretend in order to give that impression. I recognized that I was not in integrity with the person I want to be and know I'm capable of being. So I used my love of writing and self-discovery to explore the root of that. Beyond that need to be liked and accepted, there was a desire for connection and belonging, which means that community is important to me. When I think back to times in my childhood when I felt isolated and unable to be my true self, the escapes I found from that isolation included friendship and creative activities where I could express myself. Years later, writing allowed me to build new relationships and communities where I felt safe enough to experiment with turning my truths into art and relationships built on shared values of creativity, unmasking, and truth telling.

Did you know that some plants help each other grow? According to a study by the University of Portsmouth, when you plant compatible plants near each other, they can mutually benefit from each other's attributes. The study shows that placing different types of plants close to each other can boost growth, repel pests, and even improve the flavor of your harvest. Other benefits include a "positive cascade" of effects in the environment, including supporting insect and soil life and providing a greater range of fruit types for birds and mammals.

I believe that friendship and creative community operate in a similar way. Our shared values bring us together. We come seeking connection, and we mutually benefit from each other's attributes. Feeling seen, heard, and supported creates a positive cascade, a ripple effect in the environment, as we go back to our lives inspired and overflowing, with a greater range of fruit to offer in all aspects of our lives.

Matching the Inside to the Outside

A benefit of unmasking is that we integrate all of ourselves into one empowered whole, and our fears and insecurities lose their power over us. When we don't, the things we try to hide are plot points that have an effect on the arc of our story whether we consciously incorporate them or not. I could walk around in fear that someone will ask me about my relationship with my mom or find out about my financial struggles, putting myself through all the contortions that go with that, or I could own it. How about you? What do you think you need to hide, and why? How could your life change if you didn't hide this anymore? It's okay if the answers don't come right away.

Your unmasking may start on a more surface level, like me with the makeup. What are the external masks you wear, and why do you wear them? What are the inner parts you are compensating for? What would you do if you felt completely comfortable and safe and empowered to embody your whole true self? You can simply sit with these questions or write them down in your journal. There's no need to rush to conclusions. You can slow down, get curious, and start paying attention.

Even if you don't consciously slow down, life will seek your attention. Think about moments in your life when your third face unexpectedly showed up privately or publicly. Did you feel embarrassed or empowered by it? The first time I wrote publicly on my blog about my estrangement from my mother, it felt like laying my burdens down at the altar. I got a taste of the freedom of owning my story. I replaced shame with the possibility of human connection.

I won't pretend there aren't lows that come with unmasking. It's uncomfortable. You will lose people. You will overexplain or overshare sometimes as you are figuring out the art of it. But there's a difference. Any low you experience as a result of taking off your mask with sincere intentions will ultimately progress you on your journey to designing a life where you don't have to be uncomfortable in your authenticity. There is much trust needed at this point to tolerate the discomfort. But remember what we've done so far. We've explored the possibility of different storylines. Through the lens of creative thinking, we can take a hopeless situation and find an escape door, a hidden passageway. We can fathom a version of ourselves that is just beyond where we currently are in our story arc.

Imagine that each decision you make is sending you on an adventure. Will you choose the familiar path of hiding or the unfamiliar path of full expression? Which decision will send you on an adventure that invites more of what your authentic self wants to experience? What lessons can you learn from the highs and lows of past adventures? What happens when you show up as your true self and when you do not? If the concept of authentic power speaks to you, and you believe that you are most powerful when you live your truth, how can you experiment with acting on this belief?

After college, I drifted away from the arts because there was family, work, and responsibility, and creativity was not on the list of priorities. I didn't know that I would start to shrivel and forget who I am without keeping a playground of my own. I didn't know that creativity was the source of what made me feel alive and that I couldn't get that same life from anywhere else. I didn't know that creativity is the path to home, to center, to truth. I had to get fed up with my masks to begin considering what life would be like without them. It seemed that life was offering me clues left and right, inviting me to let myself be seen.

I remember taking deep breaths as I prepared to do my first reading as a self-published author in 2014. I'd arrived at the Anacostia Arts Center in southeast Washington, DC, to participate in a showcase curated by Tiona, a writer with an infectious smile and a passionate way with words whom I'd just met but would become a dear friend and creative coconspirator. The showcase was called "See. Speak. Feel." and included a variety of writers, singers, dancers, artists, and vendors. We gathered in the Black Box Theater's intimate stadium seating for a lineup of heartfelt performances. I remember feeling so at home with these people I'd never met. Artsy people. Hearts on sleeves. It felt like a reunion with the creative community that I'd been away from for too long. I wasn't sure if I belonged there, if I had a right to call myself an artist, too, but I felt welcome, and that's what mattered. Being in this environment brought out a side of me that I was only beginning to explore.

When it was my turn, I began:

Her childhood was shaped by chaos and love.

Adored and overprotected, she was taught to study, fear God and be quiet.

Her mother heard voices that no one else could hear and saw things that no one else could see.

Self-appointed, she was the one who minded the gaps.

Cleaned up the messes.

Apologized.

Got lost in managing her mother's extremes.

She felt responsible for her mother's behavior and handily designed her existence to compensate for it.

She wanted people to feel comfortable all the time, even at her own expense.

She created a story about a broken girl with a broken mother who would grow up to live a broken life. She chose that fate and lived according to it. This is the story of her disruption.

I remembered this high. As the words poured out, I lost touch with my body, and there was only my voice—the voice I'd been afraid to use for so long. It was the return to an old world and the beginning of a new one. I knew this is where I belonged and that creative expression needed to be central to my life in order for me to heal and thrive. One word at a time, bridging the gap between who I'd been pretending to be and who I felt called to become. I ultimately learned how to take off my mask by being honest with myself privately and then publicly, first through written words, then through verbal expression. I would soon learn that it wouldn't be easy to conjure this courage when I returned to the environments that stole my voice in the first place. Habits would prove hard to break, and I would discover more assumptions and self-deceptions that would threaten to throw me off my new path.

Reflection: Peaks and Valleys

When you start to feel like things should have been better this year, remember the mountains and valleys that got you here. They are not accidents, and those moments weren't in vain. You are not the same. You have grown and you are growing. You are breathing, you are living, you are wrapped in endless, boundless grace. And things will get better. There is more to you than yesterday.

—Morgan Harper Nichols

The connection between your peaks and valleys may not seem obvious, but if you look closely enough, they reveal clues about your values. Your values are ideas and concepts that are intrinsic to who you are and what brings you fulfillment. Your values highlight what you stand for, and if you're not masking your true self, they guide your behaviors, decisions, and actions. In this exercise, you will mine your memories for peaks and valleys to highlight the values that were and were not being honored in those situations.

A peak is a positive or satisfying experience. It could be a big, flashy moment like receiving an award or promotion, traveling to a new place, or getting married. It could also be something quiet that no one else knows about but was deeply meaningful to you.

A valley is a negative or unsatisfying experience. It could be a loss or an illness, a relationship or friendship that ended, a job where you felt disrespected, or a time when you broke a promise to someone.

- Make a list of peak moments in your life when you felt most authentic, alive, and inspired. Then make another list for valley moments when you felt most distant from your truest self.
- In your peak moments, what were you appreciating? Which personal values were being honored in those experiences?
- In your valley moments, what was taken away or out of reach? Which personal values were not being honored in those experiences? What opportunities developed from those valleys?

After this exercise, you will have fresh insights on your values and how they affect the quality of your experiences. This awareness can open your eyes to new choices and alternative stories, allowing you to reconnect with your creative power. The challenge is figuring out what it takes to embody those values.

What do you do when you can see where you want to go, but taking the steps proves more challenging than you thought?

Recognizing we have masks that may be hindering us can give us the desire to take them off but not necessarily the strength to keep them off. You may realize how hiding has hurt you and still face the challenge of how to embody new behaviors and responses to invite the change you seek in your life. Self-observation creates an entry point for new ideas to bloom, but then it must be followed by consistent inspired action. Self-deception gets in the way of that.

Chapter Five

The Unreliable Narrator

Self-honesty is a key ingredient for cultivating creative power in our lives. As I reunited with my creative self and rediscovered the voice I'd lost as a child, I thought I'd been set free, but I still had blind spots hiding in plain sight. In other words, I wasn't consciously aware of it, but I was just at the beginning of discovering layers of deeper conflicts that were affecting how I moved through the world. Self-deception is an avoidance technique that I developed as a girl who told lies to cover up her mother's strange behavior and refined as a grown woman who wore masks to hide her shame. For years, my self-deceptions and delusions allowed me to skim over inconvenient truths so I didn't have to face them.

When I started writing, it became a truth serum that didn't allow me to lie to myself, a practice in self-honesty and acceptance. A tool for healing. A source of self-discovery. I believe we are wired with the interests, passions, gifts, and desires that enable us to overcome the challenges we will face in our lives, and writing is one of those offerings for me. The more I wrote, the more I connected the dots between the little girl and the woman, and I learned that you can only be as honest with others as you are with yourself. Change happens on the inside before it becomes a reality on the outside, and there are some blind spots that take longer than others to illuminate.

My calling to write gave me a creative vision. Here was an outlet that offered no guarantees but gave me hope that I could overcome my tragedy story and a rebirth was possible. Hope that using my voice instead of silencing it, I would transform my pain into purpose. No other desire or challenge had given me the courage to stop hiding. Nothing else had offered me a vehicle to express the parts of me that I denied for so long in a way that felt so promising. With creative expression as my teacher, I committed to integrating everything that had once caused me shame to find new insights that would guide the next phase of my life. When I started a blog with my friend in 2009, I had no idea where the journey would take me, but I believed the project was an answered prayer and somehow everything would fall into place. Looking back, I admire my willingness to have faith and follow my heart, but I also realize I was bringing some misconceptions from the past into my new reality.

From 2009 to 2012, I gradually redirected more and more energy from my corporate job to my creative outlet. I started my own blog, in addition to the one I had with my friend and got hired to write blog posts for beauty brands for Black women. Writing wasn't just a side hustle to me; it was a heavenly destination, an escape from the hell of feeling out of place and without purpose. During that time, I blogged about discovering self-love, a concept that the natural hair movement introduced to me for the first time. I wrote testimonies about how my physical transformations represented my inner transformations. Notes and poems about finding my voice and trusting my intuition poured out of me. I wrote missives about anxiety, depression, and my fears of developing schizophrenia. Lamentations about being estranged from my mother. Confessions about comparison, envy, rejection, and failure. Shame, guilt, and hitting rock bottom. I was exploring the themes that were helping me grow, writing what I needed to hear. Giving myself and others permission to embrace all their many layers, emotions, and experiences.

But then I would close my laptop, go back to my life, and fall back into the same old habits. Even though I was practicing courage in my writing, in my daily life I was still reflexively snapping back into the person I thought I was expected to be. Trying to be everything I've always been to everyone in my life, even when it didn't feel right anymore. The back and forth was exhausting, but somehow I thought that I'd be able to have both the transformation and the old, familiar patterns. Trying to straddle both worlds created an inner distrust that lingered in my consciousness, causing me to feel like a fraud, a feeling I tried to ignore—a blind spot that kept me from finding a way out of this cycle.

Can you recall a time when you thought you'd learned a lesson and reached a new level of awareness only to find yourself reflexively responding to life in the same old ways? If so, consider this: If you were reading a book or watching a movie and the main character found a solution to all of their problems in the middle of the book, wouldn't you expect there to be a plot twist of some sort? Wouldn't you anticipate that character to face some unexpected tests and challenges that set the stage for the rest of the story? At some point, the main character will have to show their inner changes on the outside. Similarly, in our life stories, we must embody the knowledge we gain through the choices we make and how we respond to old challenges in new ways. This is how we end unwanted cycles, move forward through our character arc, and continue to evolve.

How Self-Deception Gets in the Way

In 2013, mental health was slowly becoming more of a normalized conversation in public spaces. As a writer who had years of repressed thoughts and experiences related to mental health, I wanted to be a voice working to uplift these conversations. I remembered how alone I felt when I was growing up thinking there was no one else in the world in my situation. By sharing my story, I could do my part so that others who grew up with a mentally ill parent wouldn't feel that way. Not only did I want to change the trajectory of my own story, but also I wanted to be a cycle breaker in my family and a game changer in my community.

That year, I took a leap of faith and left my job in financial services to pursue writing full time, believing that everything would fall into place if I followed this sacred calling. I was driven by a meaningful purpose, but I was naive about what it would take to make the transition. Partnering my inner journey, which was connected to my own emotional healing, to my outer journey, which was connected to how I create my livelihood, would prove complicated.

The vulnerability of it all brought up insecurities and challenges that I hadn't faced when I was working for someone else's dream. I struggled with being seen without my masks and how naked that felt, not relying on the name of a company, school, or organization to validate me—just my authentic offering, my humanity, my stories. On top of that, the tug-of-war between motherhood and career was intense as I learned how to pace and position myself as a creative entrepreneur. Despite these challenges, I put one foot in front of the other and walked forward into the unknown. I was making some part-time income from freelance writing projects but nothing close to the salary from my job. I had some savings, but I didn't have a business plan or a strategy of any kind, which added urgency and desperation to my creative efforts. In addition to all of the fears and insecurities that were coming up, I was also putting a ton of energy into pretending that I had everything under control. Just because we take our masks off doesn't mean that we won't create new ones.

By 2015, I was out of savings and went back to working part-time in financial services, writing client communications as a contractor. I took pretty much every job, client, and opportunity that came my way during that time because, again, I didn't have a plan, and I was just thankful to be carving out my own path. Even though it was messy, it was mine, and for the first time in my life, I was writing my own story. I was convinced that becoming a successful writer would bring a better version of myself to life. A version that wouldn't flip-flop and bend herself out of shape to avoid being rejected. I would step into this new life, and it would solve my problems and give me the fortitude that I was lacking. I would find my wholeness and worth through this work. Maybe I would even find the strength to find my mother and bring her back into my life. In my mind, accomplishments would bring about the changes I wanted to see. Success would give me the right to take up space.

Misconceptions like this hid in plain sight, undetected as I put all my energy into proving myself. The progression of my writing career was a single-minded obsession, and healing took a back seat. I kept thinking that once I "made it," I would concentrate on the rest of my life. I would take better care of myself and call my family members more often, I'd put down my laptop and spend more undistracted time with my little ones. I'd become my ideal self—the one who was healed, balanced, and wise. I was on an authentic path, but it was muddy with insecurities and hidden motivations that were rooted in a need to save face. I never wanted to reveal that I didn't know what I was doing, that I was making mistake after mistake, constantly recovering from bad decisions. I wasn't viewing my mistakes as information that could be analyzed and improved on; I was sweeping them under the rug because this is what I'd been conditioned to do. I didn't yet understand that it's not the end result that changes your life; it's who you become along the way as you pursue your life callings. I didn't recognize the transformative power of the learning curves. If anything, I wanted to skip over them. I didn't know that the only way out is through.

The Unreliable Narrator

Self-deception can turn you into an unreliable narrator in your own story. An unreliable narrator is a storyteller whose version of the story is altered in some way and cannot be fully trusted. In a book or movie, the unreliable narrator may consciously withhold information from the reader, seeking to mislead them, and other times their unreliability is out of their control. It may come from ignorance or delusion. Regardless of the motivation, being an unreliable narrator is a kind of self-deception that anyone can unknowingly fall into because they are so convinced of their version of the story. Similar to our masks, self-deception keeps us stuck in patterns we don't want, and it keeps us from the lessons we could be learning from our experiences.

When we avoid being honest with ourselves—when we don't investigate what's fueling old patterns that we can't shake and the stories we're telling that don't feel true—the way we recall events, scenes, and situations serves the deceptive narrative that we've attached ourselves to for safety, validation, or whatever need we are subconsciously seeking to fulfill. So much so that we often come to believe our own falsities. Like when we tell our friends that our relationship is perfect when, in reality, we are arguing every day. Or perhaps when we are convincing ourselves that we don't have a drinking, eating, or gambling problem, that we can quit at any time.

In my case, I was all in on writing about self-discovery and transformation, but I wasn't being honest with myself about the deeper work I needed to do to embody that knowledge off the page, to bring about actual change in my relationships and endeavors. I was trying to build my dream life on a shaky foundation, an unreliable narrative. Around this time, the people I was most honest with in my life were my partner, my close friends, and my sister, but even with them I often colored things so they wouldn't worry about me. I didn't want to burden any of them with the full shakiness of my reality.

Self-deception is a form of denial that gives us a sense of control over what information we willingly accept and what information we consciously or subconsciously reject. According to the American Psychological Association, it's a defense mechanism in which unpleasant thoughts, feelings, wishes, or events are ignored or excluded from conscious awareness. We protect our ideal or familiar self-concept by being oblivious to our blind spots and ignoring our intuition.

What are some ways that you deceive yourself? Sometimes we lie to ourselves about our vices and bad habits because we don't want to give them up. We rationalize in our minds that our addictions and unhealthy attachments are not a problem. We tell ourselves misleading stories about our affairs, our relationships, and our true needs and desires. We may lie to ourselves about our well-being, about how happy or sad or stressed we really are.

Doesn't it make sense that we need to be honest with ourselves in order to live our most fulfilled lives? Why do we ignore that knowing? Aspirational truth is a beautiful way to create new visions, but it can be misleading if we are not being honest with ourselves and accepting where we are right now. Anywhere in your life where you are feeling one thing but saying or doing another is a place to look for self-deception, shadows, and blind spots. As always, we can initiate self-discovery by asking ourselves heart-opening questions. If you silence the external noise and get quiet enough, you will hear questions like: *Why did I just say that when I know it's not true? What am I holding back, and why? What habits, conversations, situations, relationships, and dynamics don't feel right in my body, my gut, my soul?*

You may feel resistance to these questions at first, and that's okay. But opening up and listening is always a powerful start. Reclaiming your story is dependent on radical self-honesty and your willingness to move beyond the illusion of who you think you need to be into who you truly are. If you are your own unreliable narrator, perhaps you are trying to fake it 'til you make it, or you're trying to stay positive and "be strong" for others by ignoring your difficulties. Whatever your reason, you're doing the best you can. It's important to remember that before we move forward.

You Can't Build a New Story on Hidden Truths

Lying is an escape I learned at an early age. As far as I could tell, people didn't want my truth. They only wanted to hear what made them feel comfortable. In my home, I saw truth telling lead to gaslighting, punishment, and conflict, so I lied to keep the peace. I altered the truth to protect feelings and calm the tension. I lied to make myself seem bigger or to make myself seem smaller—whatever the situation required. I also lied to myself by not acknowledging how much it hurt to live this way. Perhaps the deception started with lies I told to cover up my mother's behavior and fill the gap of my father's silence on the matter. With no explanations provided to me, I created fearful ones forged in shame and denial. When we are under the influence of shame, we often complicate our relationships and circumstances by spinning stories to hide the truths we don't know how to face.

As I was finding my way in this new career, I was lying to myself about all the things that were falling through the cracks. And while I kept trying to fake it 'til I make it, I was in denial about how the dissonance was affecting my mental health. It's hard to say exactly when, but I think I started losing hope in 2016. I'd been self-employed since 2013, and after three years of trial and error, I thought I was finally hitting my stride. That January, I declared it a year of abundance. I hosted more writing workshops than any other year up to that point. I was invited to speak at more conferences and groups than ever before.

I had money from client contracts coming in and one-on-one coaching and ghostwriting clients keeping me busy. My kids were growing up, and I was able to be at home with them while doing work I loved.

Despite my declaration, inside I felt like I was failing. The problems I had before I changed careers persisted, and new ones emerged. I was chronically overwhelmed, and when I spent quality time with my kids, I was often distracted. My father was in the throes of dementia, and we were experiencing the long goodbye. Being unable to afford the care he deserved made me feel useless. I was still struggling emotionally and financially, and I didn't understand why. I probably could have benefited from a business coach, but I didn't know how to manage my money, so I couldn't afford one. My body was speaking to me through aches, pains, and inflammation. I didn't want to integrate these worries into my story, so I pushed them down and worked harder, believing that would solve everything.

My ambition was loud, and I was eager for results, so I didn't make time for the healthy habits that could have helped me think more clearly. I just charged ahead, avoiding any structure that might slow me down. When I started losing hope, I thought maybe I should go back to therapy, but I didn't make time. When my thoughts got darker and more troubled, I knew how to redirect them, but I allowed them to seduce me. When sadness closed in, I thought maybe I should be careful, tread lightly, but I didn't. I refused to repair or even look at the cracks in my foundation; all I wanted to do was build. That year was abundant indeed, full of experiences, opportunities, and warning signs that I ignored. The truth brings us the nourishment that our souls need, even when it doesn't necessarily taste good, and without it, we are malnourished. No matter how abundant we might look to everyone on the outside, only an individual knows when they are starving from not living their truth.

In 2017, my dad died. The biggest rock bottom of my life led to an awakening: *I'm going to die one day too. Am I living well? Am I practicing courage? Could I go in peace knowing that I never considered myself worthy enough to unapologetically live my truth?* I had to admit the answer was no. It was difficult for me to process the political, economic, and racial turbulence in the world that year when I could hardly face what was happening in my own life. I wanted nothing more than to self-isolate, retreat from the chaos, and protect myself from more pain and loss. I didn't feel safe in my skin, my mind, or my country. Everything seemed to be spiraling.

A month after he died, I was in a dark place and turned to letter writing for catharsis. In an email to friends, I wrote:

> *I'm struggling to stay above water. Sometimes when it's really really bad, I go to sleep and I romanticize not waking up and that's scary. I would NEVER hurt myself, but it's my lack of hope and lack of energy for life that scares me. Some days I can pretty easily rise above it and others I can't at all. It's like there is a heavy layer of pain on me that I can't shake off. Hopelessness. It creeps into everything, even my biggest joys, my babies. Because I feel like my anxiety and fear get in the way of me being the best parent I could be to them. Something inside me sees me making the same mistakes over and over and it tells me that all I do is disappoint people and myself and it tells me that I'm hopeless and a waste of potential and when I'm weak I believe it. It's like my spirit is tired from fighting the negative thoughts. I hate bringing people down. My whole life, I've felt purposeful about being someone who brings light and hope and comfort to people so it's hard for me to admit that all of this darkness is in me and that I'm struggling with it. But maybe that is part of the problem. Too much trying to bear this by myself.*

My friends, who all had children, families, joys, and pains of their own, held this space for my truth, and we committed to a monthly gathering to spend quality time more often. This was a turning point and an example of truth telling as a portal to solutions and support. Instead of rejecting the inconvenient truths, I was laying them out to be seen by me and the people who loved me. According to research, lying requires a huge amount of brain power, which means there is less power available for other things. So this was a step toward clearing up cognitive space for me to investigate my unmet needs, get back into therapy, and start living from an even truer place.

Self-Deception Is Not Easier than Disruption

One of the reasons we avoid self-honesty is because of the disruptions in our lives that we suspect it will cause. We may lie to ourselves and others because we fear the consequences of the truth. But if you start by allowing yourself to simply get curious about it, questions will begin to open doors that have been previously closed: *If I learn to embrace my shadows as a valuable part of my story, how could that change my outlook? If I go further to show up as a fully expressed version of myself, how might this affect my relationships? How can I prepare myself for this change?*

From external forces and other characters in our stories, we face threats like disapproval, criticism, and rejection, which may make us feel justified in the stories we spin, even when we know that self-honesty is the more courageous path. But beyond the fear of consequences from others, we lie to ourselves to avoid our own internal consequences: Having to feel feelings and inner resistance that we've been compartmentalizing for years. Facing fears that we think we can't handle, like being misunderstood or disregarded, and dealing with the fallout from that. Choosing to live in alignment brings about turbulent shifts and uncharted territory that are bound to trigger brand new anxieties and sensitivities. So often, we look around at our roles and responsibilities and think that we're in too deep and we don't have the time or energy to change direction.

I was no stranger to bypassing gut feelings that threatened to be more disruptive to my life than I was prepared to handle. I had long believed that the life I'd built was fragile and speaking too loud would make the walls fall down. But life was calling me to bring the wisdom off the page and into my real world, even into the crevices that I hid from myself. On the page, I'd been weaving this tale of waking up and taking off my mask to become free and live happily ever after. And that vision was precious to me, but it wasn't the whole story. There were still more detours and reroutes, conflicts and resolutions, and by avoiding them, I wasn't doing my story justice. Wasn't this subplot worthy to be included? Weren't these complications also a beautiful part of the adventure?

Some of us will go through our whole lives keeping our truthiest truths hidden, craving release but believing we won't survive the exposure. When your heart wants to express a part of itself that it never has before, and your mind wants to talk you out of it, writing can help you connect these forces. Even the most opaque truth, when illuminated by language, has healing power. The truths that you used to deny and avoid can become clues to your personal mystery. As you read this chapter and think about the false narratives you've told yourself and others, do it with the understanding that these dishonesties are teachers, offering you insights about what you are afraid of so you know where to look for blind spots and breakthroughs.

Self-Deception and Self-Care

In 2018, I gradually started over. Cutting back on work, I put my mental health first. In the past, my ambition was often at odds with my wellness, which made it impossible to live in integrity with who I wanted to be. That needed to change, starting with my daily habits. I set the groundwork with reading spiritual books and journaling. I also incorporated talk therapy, energy work, exercise, and a cleaner diet. About halfway through the year, I told my friends I was ready to stop waiting for a worthier version of myself to emerge through some external accomplishment. I was ready to once again reimagine what's possible, and I knew my choices needed to be rooted in self-care. This sentiment would become one of the guiding principles that I would share a few years later with my creative community: *Self-care allows the fullest expression of who you are to be released.*

Self-care is all about asking yourself what your mind, body, and soul need and generously taking action to meet those needs. When we prioritize this attention, these energies work together to make us stronger, more present, and more in tune with our inner guidance. Having spent most of my life with inner conflicts, at the mercy of unwanted visceral reactions to triggers that I didn't understand, mindfulness has been at the core of my approach to self-care. In *The Body Keeps the Score: Brain, Mind, and Body in the Healing of Trauma*, Bessel A. van der Kolk says, "Mindfulness not only makes it possible to survey our internal landscape with compassion and curiosity but can also actively steer us in the right direction for self-care." To this day, I direct my clients and workshop participants to mindfulness concepts like beginner's mind to develop fresh eyes and open minds to uncover their authentic needs—which, by the way, often hide out in our blind spots and shadows because somewhere along the way, we came to believe that we're not worthy of having them met.

I remember asking myself, *How have these blind spots been serving me? What specifically am I avoiding?* I had to acknowledge how self-deception was serving the wounded part of me and how removing that veil would disrupt the relationships and situations that were still dependent on that part. This train of thoughts made my chest tighten and my breath quicken, which made me want to turn back, but I stayed with the questions. *What am I afraid will happen if I trust this divine alignment?*

What physical sensations will I have to feel in my body if I face this fear?

My self-inquiry steered me to a missing piece of my development, and that was the ability to feel, process, and express the physical sensations beneath my difficult emotions. I would need this ability to stay true to myself in trying moments when a boundary is tested or I have to go against the grain or take a risk that tests my faith. I would have to accept the difficult feelings and notice how they affect my body without reacting to them in the same old ways like numbing, denying, and avoiding. Being my whole authentic self in all my relationships and interactions would require new languages, boundaries, and assertions. I knew I needed to give myself grace as I navigated this new territory.

When I was trying to prove myself, I was waiting for a time in the future when I would feel worthy. I saw the worth in the woman I was becoming, the one I was working toward, the aspirational me. But I didn't see the same value in the current woman in the mirror, the one with the blind spots, the figuring-it-out me. Instead of believing that becoming a successful writer would bring a better version of myself to life, I asked myself, *What would it look like for me to unapologetically value who and where I am right now? What if the real success is the freedom to be my whole authentic self in every season and space I occupy?*

When You Face Your Deceptions

I went from corporate America to creative entrepreneurship still wanting to achieve external success to find my worth and solve my problems. This motivation led me astray. But I kept coming back to the creative vision that woke me up in the first place: *How can I be a truth teller who liberates others to live their truths if I can't be honest with myself?*

To be the game changer I wanted to be, I had to allow myself to be seen trying to have my humanity on display. Many of us who have lost ourselves in self-deception evolve to become the most passionate truth tellers because we've learned that self-denial leads to nothing but dead ends, we desperately want a different experience, and we are willing to learn from the disruptions that come with this change. Our willingness gives us the power to become reliable narrators who know the significance of including the most flawed aspects of ourselves in the story. Instead of looking at our blind spots as barriers, we can look at them as teachers. We can integrate the things we are in denial about and recognize the roles they play in making us who we are. This shift can usher us into a new way of being.

In her award-winning memoir *Lit*, Mary Karr says, "If you live in the dark a long time and the sun comes out, you do not cross into it whistling. There's an initial uprush of relief at first, then—for me, anyway—a profound dislocation. My old assumptions about how the world works are buried, yet my new ones aren't yet operational."

You may find yourself facing an identity crisis and feeling awkward in social environments as you experiment with being a reliable narrator, using new language to express yourself and live your truth. For example, if you're not accustomed to putting your needs first, asking for what you really want, or going against the status quo, the discomfort can be overwhelming. There will be times when you immediately question yourself because it feels so wrong. It's not unusual to have a physical reaction after setting a boundary or speaking a difficult truth.

You may face new relationship dynamics with family members, friends, coworkers, and acquaintances. Certain jokes may not hit the same way. You may get funny looks when you don't play along with conversations that go over your head or against your values. Don't be surprised to find yourself changing the subject or removing yourself from situations that don't align with who you are and what is meaningful to you. With your new awareness, aligning your thoughts, words, and actions will be more important to you than fitting in. Some of your old language and ways of avoiding your truth will feel inauthentic and won't sit right anymore, a weight you no longer want to carry.

Your dreams and goals may change. When you fully own your needs, preferences, passions, and desires, you may find that the educational or professional path you've chosen has lost its appeal as your attention turns to the inner callings that light you up from within.

If you've been out of touch with your innermost self, relying on external validation for a sense of purpose and identity, those rewards will begin to feel empty.

It's normal to feel vulnerable and need time in solitude to process these changes. You might be unprepared for all the new sensations and how intensely they arise when you stop fighting them. The courage you need to tolerate these shifts and turn vulnerability into strength is nurtured by self-care—understanding what energizes you, what drains you, and which habits and practices restore your power. We will take a deep dive into this in chapter 9. When you've spent years reacting to life in a certain way, molding a certain image for yourself, and clinging to other people's beliefs, finding your way back to your authentic self is going to take some time. Let's not mistake that time as a period of waiting. Let's look at it as a new way of living, where there is no destination, only day-to-day choices.

Reflection: Growth Is Not Linear

We do not grow absolutely, chronologically. We grow sometimes in one dimension, and not in another; unevenly. We grow partially. We are relative. We are mature in one realm, childish in another. The past, present, and future mingle and pull us backward, forward, or fix us in the present. We are made up of layers, cells, constellations.

—Anaïs Nin

We do grow unevenly, don't we? It's tempting to be hard on ourselves when old patterns show up again and again in different shapes and forms. When you set the intention to make meaning out of your experiences, you need a growth mindset and a long-term view. If you are fully engaged with life, there will always be new blind spots to discover.

To encourage creative thinking and a growth mindset, the following reflection exercise shows you how to look at an unwanted pattern in your life and notice the difference between how you responded in the past and how you are responding now. Instead of noticing the pattern and feeling discouraged, this exercise will show you how you've evolved.

Pattern

First, describe the unwanted, repeating pattern.

Then

Describe a time in the past when this showed up and how you responded. What was your inner narrative and mindset at the time?

Now

Describe the last time it showed up and how you responded. Notice the difference between how you responded then and how you're responding now. How has your inner narrative and mindset evolved? Take notes about how you've grown as well as how you still have room to grow.

Your ability to think creatively thrives when you take care of yourself—mind, body, and soul. What *taking care* means for each person is unique, and there is much value in defining this for yourself. When we think creatively, we can imagine how our blind spots and challenges can become assets. Often, a person's greatest strength, the thing that makes them feel the most purposeful and connected, is a blind spot before it becomes a source of power. We will explore this connection more in the next chapter.

Chapter Six

Strengths and Superpowers

Three months before COVID-19 shut down the world, I walked into a classroom at the Writer's Center in Bethesda, Maryland, and took in the space where I would be facilitating my workshop. In the center of the room, there were three rectangular tables pushed together to comfortably seat about fifteen people with plenty of elbow room to write.

It was January 2020, and the event was called Mental Illness through a Literary Lens. I would be leading the group in writing stories about how mental illness had directly or indirectly affected their lives, creating candid narratives that reduce stigma and stereotypes. There I was, aligning with my why, advocating for mental health awareness through creative expression and storytelling. This opportunity was a manifestation of this intention, a wink from the universe.

Weeks earlier when I got the list of the other facilitators and panelists for this event, the first thing I noticed was that they all had more credentials and experience than me. Initially, imposter syndrome reared its head, and I was intimidated, but I was no stranger to that feeling, having encountered it many times on my writing journey. So when I found myself questioning and comparing myself, I was ready to disregard it as an annoying distraction. My path in the literary world was not paved with a writing degree, bylines, or awards, but I had the heart and the fire in me to blaze my own path, and I knew that was powerful in its own way.

I have tried to hide my heart for most of my life. It always seemed to beat too loudly and break too easily. I've seen the world as a place that doesn't cooperate with sensitive souls like me. I've suspected that I am having a different experience than everyone else and that most people didn't understand or care about my heart-centered, soul-focused point of view. I've collected evidence: people rolling their eyes or exchanging knowing looks with each other when my innocence would rear up and show itself in a whimsical comment or a sudden rush of tears. Every time I have the opportunity to facilitate a workshop or share space with a group of open hearts and minds, I revel in the reality that I am speaking from a vulnerable part of me that I used to perceive as cringy and embarrassing.

That didn't stop my stomach from flip-flopping as I got dressed that morning in my standard turtleneck-and-jeans writer uniform, as I drove the twentyish miles to get there, or as I walked into that empty room. My inner narrative bounced from critic to coach and back again the whole time:

Critic: *What if the other facilitators are cliquish and don't welcome me? What if no one comes to my session? What if I'm so nervous that I stutter and stumble over my words?*

Coach: *Enough! You belong. You were invited to do this for a reason. You have a message someone needs to hear. Just let your soul speak for you.*

My hands shook as I placed a handout at each seat around the table. I chose a seat facing the door so I could see everyone come in, and I sat down to wait, listening to my heartbeat, sipping water, my notes spread out before me.

As each person walks in, I greet them with a smile and a hello. As we introduce ourselves, I look at each person as someone who chose to be there, to let their guard down in a room of strangers and write about intimate details from their lives. I see my writing friend Anisa there, smiling and supporting, her presence another wink from the universe. As the tables fill up, my energy shifts away from my neuroses, and I focus on the environment that I want to create:

Critic: What if this exercise doesn't inspire them to write? What if this is not what they were expecting? What if I am not enough?

Coach: It is your responsibility to make this an affirming experience, to make the writers feel comfortable, seen, and heard. This is your zone. This is where your ego fades and your spirit shines.

It was a group of willing, open-minded writers—a variety of ages, backgrounds, and writing levels. A ninety-minute escape into the world of memories we don't talk about and truths we don't admit, and we all left with each other's generous offerings—our stories. Each one is a seed planted. Each one a source of courage for the entire group. It didn't matter what credentials any of us had because we weren't there to impress each other; we were there with a shared desire to write our truths out of hiding.

After the workshop, several writers came up to talk and ask questions about writing and truth telling and fear. My responses were all a version of the same message:

The key to overcoming your fears is connecting to a *why*, a deeper purpose.

You need to have a *why* that is bigger than your fear.

Your *why* fuels the courage you need for fuller expression and transformation.

Your *why* is the intrinsic motivation behind what you do and how you go about doing it.

This wisdom does not just apply to writers. Many of us begin self-discovery work in search of personal meaning, and that alone is a compelling purpose that challenges the fears that hold us back from living our truths in all its shapes and forms.

But when it comes to the actions we must take to live *inside* of this why and express it, many of us become paralyzed by the fear of being judged and criticized.

There is a touchiness around authentic expression, a deep fear of being rejected, abandoned, or hurt when revealing our vulnerabilities and differences, especially when it comes to sensitive topics like mental illness and trauma, anything that has caused us pain and suffering. When you reclaim your story, you are exercising your ability to deviate from the scripts and norms that society has imposed on you. You are discovering a novel language so you can navigate the world in a new way. What an improvement it can make in our lives when we assign our own meaning to our circumstances. When we do, no one can take that power away from us.

Owning Our Differences

If you could see into my mind, you'd find me paying more attention to the invisible currents in my environment than the visible happenings. Sometimes I'm so busy noticing the vibrations around me that I completely tune out of conversations, only to return and discover that I have missed the instructions or the punch line or the social cue. It's been unnerving to drift off into my inner world so easily without any understanding of how to control myself. Why was I so irresistibly drawn to the deep end? Why couldn't I keep my feet on the ground? It seemed that life would be easier if I could.

They call me naive. They call me quiet. In the words of Junot Diaz in *This Is How You Lose Her*, "She's sensitive, too. Takes to hurt the way water takes to paper." It's a certain softness, a fragility that has brought me great joy as well as great sadness. With that softness came little to no control over my emotional highs and lows. Being a sensitive little girl who is swept into ecstasy by the church choir and whose heart bleeds at the sight of someone suffering. Then becoming a sensitive teenager who escapes into books and art while internalizing her mentally ill mother's demoralizing accusations. Evolving into a sensitive adult who finds comfort in delusion as a connection to her mother and thinks it's her duty to bear the weight of the world. How many times have I asked myself, *What is wrong with me?* when I found myself shattered by a haphazard comment or hating myself over an honest mistake.

For a long time, I saw this sensitivity as a dangerous indication that there was something in me that could be easily broken. All the pain in the world might one day swallow me, or all the joy in the world might make me float away. I figured losing touch with reality must be just around the corner. Surely I had some kind of mental or emotional disorder that would inevitably lead to a complete psychological breakdown.

A few years ago, I discovered Dr. Elaine Aron, a pioneer in studying sensitivity, who gave me language and started me on a journey of understanding my way of being. A highly sensitive person (HSP) is a neurodivergent individual with an increased central nervous system sensitivity to physical, emotional, or social stimuli. HSPs are deeply intuitive and easily overstimulated by our environments, which can make us prone to feelings of anxiety. In 2018, I was diagnosed with generalized anxiety disorder, which is a mental health disorder that produces fear, worry, and chronic overwhelm. It is characterized by excessive, persistent, and irrational fears about everyday things. It manifests in people in different ways, but essentially you are worrying constantly and can't control it. In 2022, I was diagnosed with attention-deficit/hyperactivity disorder—inattentive type, which causes difficulty with organization, concentration, planning, time management, working memory, and the ability to finish tasks. All of this is connected to having a sensitive nervous system, which can also be attributed to or at least complicated by complex post-traumatic stress disorder (CPTSD).

Before I had language for these things, I didn't know how to explain or express my differences, which is all they are—differences. I saw them as problems, signs of my damaged existence. Before I learned that I could reclaim my story and find meaning in these challenges, my tragedy story was my default. With that mindset, my sensitive nervous system was a weakness, my fragile mental health was a weakness, and my attention disorder another weakness, all factors that made it unsafe to be myself and that I would need to overcome or hide in order to be successful.

But in that classroom where I shared my story with my fellow writers, and in that theater where I did my first book reading, and in every opportunity I've had to share my story along the way, my efforts have shown me that my sensitive nature is not something I need to overcome but something I need to embrace and use to help others embrace their differences too.

What I have learned now after years of facilitating writing workshops and groups is that there is power in being sensitive to nuances that others don't notice. There is power in being candid and speaking from the heart. This is something I am uniquely qualified for, being a sensitive soul with a love of words and meaning and expression, but when I was in my tragedy story, I had a victim mentality that was fixed on the belief that my softness could not possibly be a strength. My calling to write led me to be a voice for mental health awareness and a cycle breaker in my family, and that purpose became bigger than my fears.

We have a choice to be empowered or disempowered by our differences. Perhaps you, too, have a quality, condition, or characteristic that if you moved the lens a few degrees in another direction, you might be able to see anew. Often your greatest strength, the thing that allows you to feel the most purposeful and connected in life, is a source of insecurity and suffering until you learn to find the value in it.

Empowered or Disempowered

The way we respond to our differences affects how our stories unfold. I could not have found the courage to publish books, facilitate workshops, and coach people in self-discovery and expression if I hadn't learned to value my sensitivity and do something with it other than feel burdened. One way to turn a perceived weakness into a strength is to ask yourself: *What special powers could be hidden here? How can I embrace the advantages of this quality and manage the challenges? How can I turn it into something useful?*

In *Big Magic: Creative Living beyond Fear*, author Elizabeth Gilbert says, "The universe buries strange jewels deep within us all, and then stands back to see if we can find them." Sometimes we mistake our strange jewels for skeletons in our closets. What if, instead, we pulled the vulnerable aspects of ourselves out of the closet with the perspective that every challenge hides a treasure?

Travel back in your life to a time when your mind wasn't limited by what's realistic and practical. Imagine being open enough to believe that you have superpowers and the only way to learn how to use them is to go on a journey of self-discovery. This journey includes twists and turns, pivots and detours, and you will encounter both predators and guides along the way. On that journey, you will make observations and study patterns, you will get lost, and you will have to face your weaknesses before you find the right path, but it will be a treasure hunt leading you to those strange jewels, unexpected gifts, and the mastery of your superpower.

Yes, we all have superpowers, but not all of us are willing to take the journey to discover them. I remember watching the Care Bears as a little girl and believing that I, too, had the power to radiate a beam of love and light from my chest to the people around me to bring calm to any situation, to awaken kindness in others, to attract good people and repel bad people. Unlike the Care Bears, my beam of light was invisible, but that didn't affect my conviction that this was something true and special about me. I could feel the power in my chest, my eyes, my voice and body, but I didn't always know how to wield it, and often fear would cause me to lose control of it. Later in life, after years of believing that I am too naive, too sensitive, I would reflect on this to remember this little girl who was intuitively aware of her strengths and wholeheartedly believed in them. We need to awaken that belief to rediscover our creative power.

Turning Weaknesses into Strengths

What is different about you that seems to make life harder for you? Which events have caused you to feel broken, damaged, or limited? What have you been made to believe is possible or not possible because of it? The beginning of turning weaknesses into strengths is to get curious about what value those so-called weaknesses hold for you. As a creative coach and facilitator, I teach people how to commit their life experiences to paper in a way that highlights their personal transformations and supports their healing, personal growth, and creative pursuits. We look for the wisdom, lessons, and gifts that were born from the challenges they've faced. There are countless ways to frame any situation, and it's important that we consciously choose. I asked a few of my clients to reframe something they once viewed as a weakness, and this is what they said:

> Max said that she felt lost as a mother to three sons on the autism spectrum and was feeling alone with her struggles. She started a blog to share her experiences, and soon a support group was born, a place where she could connect with other mothers who had children on the spectrum so they could have a safe space to be open about their challenges. She turned isolation into community.

Carla said that one day she was walking home from work, and she left the main road to take a shortcut through a familiar wooded area. On that particular day, someone followed her into the woods and sexually assaulted her. In the days and weeks after, she carried a great sense of shame. She developed the idea that she should just hide the experience away within herself, and that would be that. Eventually, she went to therapy, where the therapist gave her a reframe that freed her: She didn't have to hide away this part of her life and let it fester and poison her. Rather, like a tree, with its knots and bumps and varied directions, she, too, could embrace what happened to her as part of what shapes who she is. She turned shame into self-love.

Amanda said that for much of her life, she felt like something was wrong with her brain. She found it hard to pick up on things quickly, to remember small details or the specifics of what someone said, and to translate her thoughts into words quickly. If she's trying to learn something in a formal setting, she gets distracted if the teacher seems upset or annoyed or if there is something going on with other students. This level of emotional intelligence would leave her nervous system feeling raw at times, but she reframed her critical view by noticing how her sensitivity serves her in so many other ways. For example, with her children, she is often able to pick up on their indirect communication around their needs. She is also able to read a room and figure out the best way to connect with people.

In each situation, rather than staying fixed in the belief that their circumstances were impossible to overcome, they looked for life lessons that could add value to their own lives and others. They looked for a meaning that built them up rather than breaking them down. What do your differences enable within you? What life lessons have you learned while managing the challenges that come with them?

In that classroom at the Writer's Center, I asked the brave souls in my workshop to transform their mental health challenges into artful narratives, so no matter what they've been through, their stories can be sources of strength and wisdom. When we do this, we are on our way to becoming the hero of our own stories.

From Victim to Hero

In his book *Hero on a Mission: A Path to a Meaningful Life*, author Donald Miller says that in stories, there are four primary characters: the victim, the villain, the hero, and the guide. The book states, "The Victim is the character who feels they have no way out. The Villain is the character who makes others small. The Hero is the character who faces challenges and transforms. The Guide is the character who helps the hero."

We have all played the victim character at one time or another, and many of us get stuck in that mindset, not realizing the options that could be revealed through a broader perspective. Accordingly, we find ourselves in a tragedy storyline where we believe that fate is in control and we have no choice but to go along with it. Under the spell of our shortcomings, differences, traumas, and struggles, we might decide that life is all meaningless and unfair; we may beat ourselves up or blame others, complain or make excuses, not realizing that we have the power to influence our circumstances.

Miller says, "All we need to know to fix our stories are the principles that make a story meaningful. Then, if we apply those principles to our lives and stop handing our pen to fate, we can change our personal experience and in turn feel gratitude for its beauty, rather than resentment for its meaninglessness."

The principles he refers to include taking action toward a purpose and having a positive attitude toward the adversity that we are all bound to face. Victims believe they are doomed, so they don't take action. They don't look within themselves for possibilities, and they might believe that their only hope is to be rescued or to have their problems magically erased. The victim resigns themselves to being disadvantaged by their differences and at the mercy of their circumstances. There's a fixed mindset here that believes that one's limitations can't change or be interpreted in a different way, so when it comes to turning weaknesses into strengths, victims don't recognize their opportunities to evolve.

Miller says that a victim becomes a villain when they don't process their pain, and they take it out on other people. You might think you have no traces of villain energy, but everyone does, even if it's subconscious. The more we take action and make choices with that energy, the more pain we experience. If you find yourself being envious of others who seem to have it easier than you, or acting out against others to control your environment, or recreating the same negative situations for others that have been created for you, those are signs that you are in this place. They say that hurt people hurt people. A villain is a victim who has not learned how to transform their pain into something useful, and they either directly or indirectly bring pain to others.

Victims and villains are stuck in disempowering patterns. Heroes transform their pain into purpose and meaning that drive their story forward. A hero is a main character who turns their weaknesses into strengths and their strengths into superpowers by going on a mission, motivated by the desire to find purpose, a calling they believe in. The challenges they face draw out the strange jewels that make them grow stronger, wiser, and more adaptable.

Many heroes awaken to their power with the help of a guide. According to Miller, guides are wise heroes who lead others out of victimhood and into being the hero of their own lives. They pass on their knowledge as a way to give back and contribute to the story of us all. They do this with the kind of care and compassion that can only come from someone who has suffered in some way too. The guide knows how to make meaning from their pain and feels a responsibility to help others do the same.

In what ways have you been the hero of your own life by transforming pain into purpose? What guides have set an example or provided inspiration for you, either directly or indirectly? How did their guidance expand your vision of what's possible?

Turning Strengths into Superpowers

Once you turn weaknesses into strengths by identifying the value they hold for you, you then use discernment to choose safe spaces to experiment. As you step into your strengths, you will gravitate toward people and situations where you connect on the level that once made you feel isolated. You become each other's witnesses, vision holders, cheerleaders, and expanders. There's no denying the nourishment that comes from finding the right community. If you even have one person—a partner, friend, family member, therapist, pen pal, and so on—you are giving yourself that safe space where you can build courage and confidence.

I gravitate toward artists, writers, and creative types because they wear their hearts on their sleeves. My empathy became a superpower by putting myself in creative environments where sensitivity is safe, vulnerability is generosity, and people value the alchemy of expression. By connecting with other humans who share these values, I put my reframe into action—centering my sensitivity as a strength that allows me to awaken the hidden strengths in others. You must know that as you awaken to your strengths, you will draw some people to you, and others will drift away. You can trust this alignment. Being a clear channel of who you are and what matters to you naturally attracts the people and relationships that nurture the strengths you are developing. The community you build creates an ecosystem of wisdom and emotional support where you can spread your wings.

When your story of differences or disadvantages becomes a source of strength, you know you've turned a corner because you are recognizing the value and you are utilizing the wisdom. It becomes a superpower when you have also found ways to manage the challenges that come with it. With great power comes great responsibility. To harness our power, we must be resourceful in finding techniques and tools that support us in our quest for healing and development.

I turned to mindfulness, the modality that has accompanied me on my healing journey every step of the way. The modality that taught me about attention without judgment. I know now that being highly sensitive is a benefit to my creativity because of how I find inspiration in the entire spectrum of human emotion from deep joy to profound sadness, and I see the possibility for creative interpretation in all of it. I naturally hold space for what others are experiencing and care about creating harmonious environments, which is beneficial in my work as a facilitator. However, the ability to sense the emotions of others can become distracting and exhausting. For years, I was controlled by my moods and permeable to the energy around me without any idea of how to control the give and take.

To manage that dynamic, mindfulness in the form of meditation helped me learn how to manage my emotions. I started with fifteen-minute sessions in the morning after walking my daughter to kindergarten. I'd sit crisscross on the floor next to my bed, close my eyes, and slow down my breathing. On the inhale, pulling the air down, down until my belly gets big and then releasing through my mouth and repeat. Fifteen-minute sits turned into twenty-minute sits, sometimes in silence, sometimes to vibrational sounds or binaural beats, classical music, or guided affirmational meditations. I would often stare at my closed lids and "see" an endless highway made of light stretched out before me. Over time, I craved this pocket of the day when I was able to let everything go and center myself in love.

Meditation has had a cumulative effect on the state of my nervous system and how I stay grounded through change. When you don't have a practice to quiet your mind, it goes and goes all day long from one thought to another, one reaction to another. In a constant state of outward attention, our minds can become overstimulated, particularly for those of us with sensitive nervous systems. Through meditation, you can find open space, an inner stillness that comes from letting thoughts pass through your mind without reacting to them. In releasing your attachment to your thoughts, you're learning a skill that you can use even when you're not meditating, an ability to practice greater discernment about what you absorb and what you let go, what you respond to and what you ignore. Meditation creates space for creative impulses and fresh insights, quieting the room of your mind so intuition can be heard. The answers to challenges reveal themselves in the stillness you cultivate for yourself through meditative practice. Meditation gently awakens your spiritual potential, so you can harness the mysterious gifts that our life experiences offer.

No matter what challenges you are facing, there is bound to be some mental chatter in your mind that gets in the way of higher instincts and impulses. Meditative practices ease that inner chatter, and it doesn't have to be just meditation; it can be any activity that calms and settles your mind. Expansion can also come from resources like therapy, coaching, breath work, yoga, and other modalities depending on your needs and inclinations.

Through years of continuous mindfulness practice, mostly in the form of meditation, journaling, and walking, I found an increased ability to manage my energy and emotions, dismiss intrusive thoughts, and access my gifts. When your strengths become superpowers, you trust yourself and your resources. That is how you'll know. You've found this place inside where your inner power is clear and pure, independent of praise and criticism. Adversity will alter your life path, but your story will become someone else's inspiration. Imposter syndrome will show up when you are pursuing your goals, but you will activate your inner coach to put it in its place. You will face beginnings and endings and turning points where you are searching for meaning, and you will look inside to remember your why or discover a new one. You will become weary at times, and you will have supportive practices, relationships, and communities that refill your cup.

In the past, there was always a voice in my head telling me that I'm not enough, and listening to that voice, I often interpreted situations in my life to be evidence of it. Becoming a coach and facilitator has been a huge part of turning my perceived weaknesses into strengths because it taught me how to let go and connect with my audience in a pure and unfiltered way, trusting that my soul will speak through me and reach the souls that are open to it. With my story as my strength and my vision to support people in the discovery and expression of their stories, I was able to put my insecurities aside and be driven by this purpose.

Reflection: Our Differences Are Divine

> *Vulnerability sounds like truth and feels like courage. Truth and courage aren't always comfortable, but they're never weakness.*
>
> —Brené Brown

Our differences allow us to offer authentic value and one-of-a-kind energy. Contrary to what society conditions us to believe, what makes us different gives us strength. A weakness becomes a strength when we recognize the value in it. A strength becomes a superpower when we learn to lean into the benefits and manage the challenges. No matter what our specific gifts are, the universal power here is the ability to turn our weaknesses into strengths and harness our strengths to move our stories forward, creating a meaning that we are inspired by and that fuels us with purpose.

Think about sci-fi movies where the character has a superpower, and they must learn how to use it or lose everything they hold dear. Our circumstances may not be life or death, but our greatest strengths can be dismissed as weaknesses if we don't learn to understand, embrace, and control them. Without the strength that comes from the wisdom of our experiences, we are less equipped to face life's challenges and be a source of strength for our families and communities.

But when you lean into your hero energy, your strengths become superpowers. Your superpower is a unique quality that gives you a heightened awareness of certain things, an edge or ability. Maybe your superpower is sensitivity or empathy. Your superpower could be a competency for recognizing patterns or creating systems. Perhaps you are charismatic and can talk your way into or out of anything. Maybe your superpower is maintaining a hopeful state of mind through illnesses, setbacks, and misfortunes. You might be a master storyteller with the ability to offer the perfect story at just the right time. We find our strengths in our willingness to explore our natural abilities, even the ones that sometimes feel like a burden.

What characteristics, gifts, and abilities come naturally to you but have felt like a burden to carry? The following exercise will help you build confidence in your differences by knowing them from all sides:

- First, make a list of personal characteristics or circumstances that make you different or have caused you to feel different from your family or peers in the past.
- Next to each one, identify the strengths and benefits of that characteristic, as well as the weaknesses and challeng-

es. By doing this, you are getting to know this trait from all different sides, including the shadow side.

- The last step is to journal about actions you can take to support the strengths and manage the weaknesses.

It bears repeating that no matter what you're facing, the universal challenge is the ability to transform pain into something purposeful. Victims don't see the benefit of pain. Heroes find something meaningful in it that can be useful to themselves and others. We must take the thing that has hurt us and transform it into inner strength.

Eventually, we will face a time when we need to use this power to cope with grief and loss, inevitable parts of life that test our faith and ability to think creatively.

Chapter Seven

Nothing Is Ever Lost

Our stories are shaped by beginnings and endings. It's our responsibility to keep our arms open for the entirety of the experience and accept the conflicting emotions that reside together as we face each moment, each day, each season in our lives. At any given time, life may have us grieving and celebrating, dreading and anticipating, longing for the past while looking forward to the future. Life is both/and, not either/or. When our emotions battle, we wonder if the turmoil will pull us into a labyrinth we can't escape. But the more we make room for what hurts, the more we make room for what heals. It is safe and necessary to acknowledge our extremes because the fact that they exist makes them true, and acknowledging what's true is always liberating, even when the truth doesn't initially feel good. Regret and acceptance, grief and joy, disappointment and resilience, destruction and creativity—how do we embrace the extremes and trust that we can handle whatever comes? How do we hold hope and loss in the same hand?

You and I have been journeying together through the origins of our stories and the pathways we have taken, and while I want for you to be feeling newfound hope and expanded creative vision, you might also be experiencing unexpected feelings of loss. Regret over lost time. Lost opportunities and relationships. Lost energy that could have been channeled in a better way. Loved ones who are gone and don't get to see you evolving. As I heal, I can't help but look back at seasons of my life when I was lost and disoriented, neglecting all the blessings and potential in my life because I was so preoccupied with what seemed lacking. My mind produces an image of my younger self—her smiles, tears, and hungry eyes—and my heart breaks over how I used to betray her, allow her to settle for scraps, and repeatedly self-destruct. Regret emerges as grief, an echo of shame, a series of intrusive memories that haunt me. I grieve who I could have been. I grieve those missed opportunities to trust my inner compass, to say yes to what felt right and no to what felt wrong. My mind quantifies how much I have lost. But when I think with my heart, I know there has been more joy than pain.

As we go through life, we make choices, we learn, we stretch, and along the way, we release the versions of ourselves that we've outgrown. We release the mindsets that once protected us and helped us survive. We release the paths we didn't take. We experience the bittersweet: peace and conflict, dreams and nightmares, wins and losses. The ability to accept the bitter with the sweet is a practice, and life is an ever-willing teacher. Since I was a child, I have been terrified of loss, and I've been grieving for as long as I can remember. Good times always find me with a layer of melancholy under the surface as I watch precious moments come and go. Susan Cain, author of *Bittersweet: How Sorrow and Longing Make Us Whole*, describes the state of being bittersweet as "a tendency to states of longing, poignancy, and sorrow; an acute awareness of passing time; and a curiously piercing joy at the beauty of the world. The bittersweet is also about the recognition that light and dark, birth and death—bitter and sweet—are forever paired."

Every life includes love and loss. We need to know it's okay to grieve our losses; in fact, it's vitally important to make room for grief in our stories so we can live wholeheartedly, not in fear of what we might lose. We fear grief because it's a black hole that we don't understand. Grief lays you bare and leaves you grasping for who you were and what you had before the loss, and it can haul you back to the scarcity mindset of a victim. When grief demotes me to the tragedy storyline and its narrow rhetoric—the time I've wasted, the people I've hurt, the people who are gone, the things I never said, the time I didn't get to spend—I notice that this train of thought isn't a resting place for me anymore. It comes from a time when I lived as if my story were complete and there were no more choices to be made. By allowing myself room to grieve, I still encounter those thoughts, but my imagination has blossomed into a guiding light that won't let me wallow in loss for too long without uncovering some meaning. I know now that while I can't change the past, there are more chapters to the story.

To hold hope and loss in the same hand, we need to open our minds to a different relationship with impermanence and grief. We cannot avoid loss. We lose loved ones; we experience grief about relationship breakups, loss of health and financial security, job loss, religious disillusionment, and more. As we peel back the layers of loss in this chapter, proceed with care. Grief is a dense topic, so pay attention to what it stirs up in your emotional and physical body. I promise to lead you to the potential for grief to become an opening for change and transformation, for loss to become a source of motivation in your life.

We can't talk about grief without talking about love. Let's ponder this connection and explore how beginnings, endings, and impermanence shape life and how loss affects the way we live and the stories we tell ourselves. We will ask ourselves, *How can I look at loss differently, as if nothing is ever lost, only transformed? What if the grief we experience could be used as guidance in how to live? How can I turn grief into something that nourishes the soul?*

All along I Was Grieving

My father was a gentle giant with large, indestructible hands. His rough hands sorted mail at the post office to provide for us, and he used them to paint, sculpt, build, and fix things in his spare time. He spent his weekdays in blue Dickies uniforms, and he was content to spend most weekends visiting with family and friends, working around the house, or yelling at the TV while watching World Wrestling Entertainment. I remember evenings as a little girl coming home from hanging out with my mom, walking into the family room to find him reclining on the couch with one long, fuzzy arm up outstretched along the back. I'd amble over to him and nestle myself right into that spot, cozy in the pit of his arm, safe in his scruffiness, the most comfortable rock I would ever know.

But those moments ended, and our relationship was strained after that day when I stumbled into the bathroom at the wrong time and my mother began to sexualize our bond. I started keeping my distance from him when she was around, walking on eggshells, carefully strategizing my words and movements. Eventually, my mother didn't want us in the house alone together at all, so she made arrangements for me to go to my best friend's house after school, and she'd pick me up on her way home from work. As much as this distance hurt my father and me, we never discussed it. Our sadness was absorbed by the silence that governed our household, strengthening its heavy-handed grip.

Even with the imposed distance between us, he quietly continued being my dad. We always had to have a good reason for my mother to accept the two of us going out alone, so he would take me to school, shopping, or to doctor's appointments, and after those errands, we would squeeze in family visits that she wouldn't approve of. My mother was suspicious of everyone, so I rarely got to see my siblings from my dad's first marriage or my cousins, aunts, and uncles on either side of my family. But Dad found ways for me to spend time with them. New Year's Eve at Nana's house in the Hill District with my cousins. Bumpy rides up cobblestone hills in Homewood to visit my maternal grandmother, Grandma Yum-Yum, named for her delicious cooking. Lunches and outings with my sophisticated older sister, Lynn, when she was visiting from New York or London or whatever cool city she was living in at the time. When I got older, he's the one who taught me how to drive, and he's the one I went to when I wanted to get on birth control. And when my grade point average dropped and I lost my scholarship after freshman year at Morgan State, I thought I would have to transfer to an in-state school at home to save money, but he helped me pay the out-of-state tuition so I could stay where I was. He helped me escape even though we never discussed what I was escaping from.

He showed his love through acts of service, but the one thing he could never give me was a direct conversation about what happened to us, to our family, in words—my love language. I grieve this absence of communication and the generational healing that could have helped both of us move on with more peace of mind and understanding. For a long time, I felt emotionally abandoned by my dad because he never asked how my mother's illness affected me. As I got older, I understood that he didn't have the words or cultivation to do that, and so I learned to reflect on what he *did* have, what he gave so generously, and what his acts of love said to me. There I found the imprint of his character, the values that shaped him, the expression of his intentions.

In the late '90s and early 2000s, as my mother moved mentally and physically farther away—first to New York, then to Miami—my relationship with my father evolved, and what he couldn't give me in words, he gave me in his presence and example. How he continued to care for my mother long after they were divorced, calling me to ask about her, worried that she didn't know anyone in these "dangerous cities" and that people would take advantage of her. Worried that she wouldn't have enough money or be able to cash the checks he sent her: "*Is there a PNC Bank there? Where will she do her banking?*" How he drove from Pittsburgh to Maryland for all my kids' birthdays every year, even when the drive made his knees ache. He made every effort to be present, and although he never said it, I think the time we lost was heavy on his mind too. Without stating it, we both were soothed by turning the bitterness of loss into the sweetness of second chances.

We were on the phone one day in 2012 when his words started to slur and trail off at the end of his sentences. I called my sister, who called my aunt, and by the end of the day, my father was in the hospital recovering from a stroke, and we learned that he'd been diagnosed with Parkinson's disease months ago and hadn't told us. I was shocked but not surprised because I knew my parents to keep secrets and avoid asking for help. As we heard his prognosis and braced ourselves, the whole time I was thinking that I wasn't ready to lose him again.

Over the next five years, we experienced the long goodbye as dementia set in and the twinkle in his eyes faded into a blank stare. We watched him lose the trappings of his independence, like paying his own bills and preparing meals for himself, as well as his curiosity, creativity, and humor, as he gradually lost interest in his hobbies and friends. My sister and I visited from our respective states during that time, but my aunt and brother did the daily caregiving until they couldn't do it alone anymore. We scrambled to find help, to educate ourselves, and to get his house in order—all while grieving. We wondered if we were making the right decisions. Through it all, I mourned the time we lost, but I also relished the time we had.

Losing my relationship with my mother and then my father, again and again, in different ways and for different reasons, became defining circumstances in my life that forced me to face my fear of loss. As my parents faded, my children grew and thrived. Life kept moving on, and I stumbled along to keep up, wishing I could slow things down and spend more time with each moment. As each day turned so quickly into yesterday, I absorbed the joy and pain, the gains and losses, the sweet and bitter. All along, I was hoping. All along, I was grieving.

Grief is a familiar companion that was with me before I knew anything about death. I started grieving the first time my mother looked at me with more suspicion than love. The grief deepened when I could no longer hug my father without worrying that I would make my mother jealous. The grief took over when I lost my innocence and began asking myself during happy moments, *When is this love going to turn into loss?* I was a young girl with an old soul, weary with the reality that change, often unwanted change, is always looming and can't be stopped. Even things you treasure most. Even love can go away without warning. With that weariness, I went through life grieving, longing for people, time, and places, relationships, versions of myself, even the ones that I hadn't lost yet.

Loss loomed as something to avoid like a punishment, a moral failing. So I ran from it, feared it around every corner. Tried to manipulate life to escape it. *Don't let it catch me. Don't let me bring it upon myself.* Loss and impermanence are subjects I couldn't confront until my father died in 2017. Since then, I've opened the door to this taboo area in my mind, with a desire to ease my fear of it. Change has shown me that everything in this world is impermanent except for love. The passage of time has shown me what it means to make grief and loss a natural part of life. While I once feared that grief would steal love away, I now recognize that grief *is* love. When I summon my values, I know that holding back love to avoid the pain of grief is not an option. I must take the bitter with the sweet to reclaim my story. To paraphrase the words widely attributed to Sufi poet and mystic Rumi, life involves both holding on and letting go. Creative expression provided a way to manage the tension between the two.

Different Forms of Loss

Western society talks about loss in a narrow, prescriptive way, and therefore we think we are supposed to experience it within specific parameters. The biggest loss, the most taboo of all, is death. In America, we are conditioned to grieve within a limited timeframe, and after the appropriate amount of mourning, we are to return to our normal—and productive—lives as soon as possible.

So we try to follow certain steps to move through grief in a linear way, checking off the boxes as we go. But if we don't do it just right, mourn just enough, and recover fast enough, then we think we are doing something wrong. Our true feelings are suppressed, which adds to our sense of isolation, even though it is such a normal and inevitable part of every life story. We see how our families, communities, and other cultures grieve, and we are influenced by the expectation and the mystery. When loss finds you, you may expect to lose your mind, wail, or collapse on the floor. But when it looks you in the eye, you may not be able to shed a tear; you may go numb or shut down. You may think you are supposed to bypass the sorrow by busying yourself with tasks or immediately get into gratitude and celebrating life. In Chimamanda Ngozi Adichie's *Notes on Grief*, she says, "We don't know how we will grieve, until we grieve."

Any expectation for how a person *should* experience grief is unreasonable; furthermore, limiting the right to grieve only to loss of life is even more unreasonable. Life is a cycle of loving and losing, learning and letting go, and we grieve many types of losses along the way. What if we gave ourselves permission to cooperate with all the ways that we experience grief and loss in our lives? If we did, we could also uncover the many creative choices we have to turn grief into gratitude.

What is loss if not change? And change is one thing that is an inevitable, unpredictable, and constant part of what it means to be alive. We lose versions and images of ourselves, seasons of our lives, and states of mind. We lose friendships, bonds we thought would never break. We lose memories and material things; we lose jobs and opportunities. We leave homes, cities, and communities behind, sometimes by choice and sometimes not. There are the roads not traveled, the chances we don't take, the unpursued dreams. Eventually, everything goes.

Societal narratives generally do not acknowledge grief outside of the death context, and even then, they disenfranchise individuals by not honoring the significance of other types of loss. Disenfranchised grief is the psychological term for when your grieving doesn't fit in with the larger society's attitude about dealing with loss. Since so many of our losses are not acknowledged, we tend to suppress our grief, and the lack of support can prolong emotional pain. Take a moment to acknowledge the role that loss has played in your emotional history and how it has informed your behaviors, decisions, and actions. Reflect on the choices and changes, beginnings, endings, and transitions. Think about the meaning you have assigned to these experiences. How has it shaped your story?

It was modeled for me to quickly move on, give it to God, don't wallow in loss, have faith. As such, I never learned how to grieve without fear and shame. When I felt the familiar earthquake rising up—when I thought about my childhood, or my parents, or anything precious that had slipped through my fingers—I would earnestly bypass it, tuck it away, willing myself to let go in order to feel better. I was afraid that sitting with my sadness, even for a spell, would allow the earthquake to swallow me whole. Even with that effort, I was only fooling myself to think I was keeping it at bay. What happens when we don't allow ourselves to experience loss in a healthy way, integrating it as a transformative part of our story? It can then become one of those fatal flaws we've talked about, a blind spot that grows in the shadows, narrowing our creative vision and limiting our options.

Grief in the Body

In our daily lives, we may not recognize that the sadness, anger, stress, and loneliness that are wreaking havoc on our well-being might be symptoms of grief. Grief is not just emotional; it is a physical experience. Grief can manifest physically in body aches, joint pain, tension, stiffness, headaches, and stomach upset. When we are grieving, our bodies produce extra stress hormones, and the elevated levels affect our cardiovascular and immune functioning and may increase inflammation in the body.

To renegotiate our relationship with loss, we need to recognize what grief feels like and how it affects us. When our minds are in denial, our bodies tell the truth. Have you ever considered that your stories don't just live in your head, that your mind is essentially a translator of what your body is experiencing? Our emotional and physical reactions are messages that our bodies communicate, letting us know we have stories inside that we need to acknowledge. Think about how your body reacts when you hear that one song that reminds you of that summer after high school graduation. How it reacts when you smell the cologne that reminds you of your favorite uncle. When you eat macaroni and cheese like your grandma used to make or when you see your ex-lover with their new partner. Depending on what your body remembers, you may realize that you are clenching your jaw or holding your breath. Tears are coming to your eyes, your heart is beating faster, or your chest feels warm with love and remembrance. Your body is telling a story, but are you paying attention?

Our bodies are time capsules, and they remember what our minds may forget. Our stories of loss and longing are alive in our nervous systems, expressing themselves in a language we can come to understand through mindfulness. This is an integral part of changing our relationship with grief, pain, and truly all difficult emotions. When we ignore pain, tension, numbness, and other discomforts in our bodies, we miss out on discovering what those signals are trying to communicate to us. Learning this language is often challenging at first because many of us live in our heads, dissociated from what's going on in our bodies. Grief is painful, and it makes sense that we are inclined to avoid the discomfort, but when you think about how numbing yourself to pain also numbs you to healing, it's worth reimagining that relationship.

Slowing down enough to notice what is happening in our bodies helps us trace the sensations back to an emotion or event or experience, an inner story that is asking for attention. Grief often leaves us at a loss for words, so once you start paying attention to how your body reacts, you may not immediately know how to translate it into verbal language. For example, when coping with loss, you may have butterflies in your stomach, tightness in your chest, muscle weakness, or a knot in your throat. You might feel nauseous or dizzy or achy. These sensations may come and go, often triggered unexpectedly by some external stimulation like a song, a smell, or a memory. In chapter 2, I shared that when my friend asked me about my parents, my heart jumped in my chest, and the ground swayed under my feet as if I was hit with an unexpected wave. Every time someone asked me about my parents, I had these visceral reactions that were embodiments of sadness, guilt, and shame. Depending on the situation I would then change the subject (flight), become defensive (fight), or start stuttering and panicking (freeze).

By noticing and describing the sensations in your body, you can connect them to your emotions, and then connect your emotions to your behavior. Some of us react to the discomfort by lashing out at people. We can't get out of bed or take care of ourselves, or maybe we busy ourselves with social engagements to avoid our feelings. Working with a professional therapist to find the connections between the sensations in your body and how you are responding to them can be helpful.

All of this is so you can name what you are feeling, so you can become aware and familiar with it, normalize it. So you can more consciously choose how to handle loss and navigate grief with awareness and self-compassion. By noticing the meaning we are assigning to our feelings and experiences, we can construct a storyline that preserves what we have lost while ushering in healing and acceptance.

Grief from All Angles

In addition to being observant about how grief shows up in our bodies, understanding how grief manifests in our lives is an important part of weaving it into our life stories in a restorative way.

Abbreviated grief is a short-lived mourning where we don't give ourselves the time we need to grieve, and we convince ourselves that we are over it before we really are. This can lead to silent grief, which involves attempting to hide our true emotions behind a mask of strength or cheerfulness. The goal is to not let others see what we are going through, to avoid pity or the feeling of being a burden. Perhaps you are "the strong one" and you feel a responsibility to uplift everyone else, so you won't let yourself surrender to feeling down.

We experience absent or delayed grief when we are shrouded in shock or denial, unable to process our emotions after a loss. Someone experiencing this type of grief may feel numb or avoid certain people and places that remind them of their loss, or they might throw themselves into their work to keep themselves occupied.

One of the most surreal parts of loss is how time keeps moving on when our personal world is still reeling. There's a desire for time to stand still while you make sense of what's happening. This can become complicated or chronic grief when you are not able to return to normal functioning for more than a year after the loss. You may require professional intervention to find your way back.

Anticipatory grief refers to experiencing the feeling of loss before the loss actually happens. I encountered this when my father was ailing with dementia. If someone in your life is ill or living a dangerous lifestyle, you may experience anticipatory grief. Or if you are someone who deals with existential dread, you may experience this kind of grieving in advance, even when everyone is fine, and you are simply hyperaware of the impermanence of things.

Cumulative grief is when you are working through multiple losses built up over time. Perhaps you had a death in your family at the same time you lost your job, and then you moved away from a town you loved. It seems that cumulative grief is inevitable given that the longer you live, the more loss you will experience. Usually associated with a series of losses within a short span of time, cumulative grief can also build up over years, particularly when we aren't actively attempting to heal.

Distorted grief is when someone gets stuck in the more intense and debilitating emotions such as anger, hopelessness, and despair. Those who are in distorted grief may seek out self-destructive coping mechanisms such as substance abuse or risky sexual behavior. They might seek revenge on someone they blame for the loss. They may also have more private manifestations like insomnia, nightmares, and suicidal thoughts.

Collective grief occurs when a community, society, or nation face a loss together. We suffer together when there are mass casualties from a natural disaster. When we are witnesses to war, genocide, and crimes against humanity that we feel helpless to stop. When a certain class, religion, or race of people is targeted and discriminated against or when we collectively mourn the deterioration of our planet and natural resources.

All of these can lead to ancestral grief, the embodiment of our ancestors' unprocessed sorrows. It can manifest as anxiety, sadness, anger, and guilt as we often unknowingly carry the trials and tribulations of generations before us. This grief can lead to limiting beliefs about our identities and our bloodline that affect how we deal with adversity and make our way in the world.

You can see how these different types of grief can overlap, and you likely have already experienced or witnessed all of these. Having the language to describe grief is reassuring, and eventually it becomes empowering as we find creative ways to move through it. When we don't have a healthy language to speak about loss, it makes us feel more alone than we really are. But when we look for the story in what is happening, we can bring to mind the natural cycle of things, make peace with it, and remember our creative choices:

What story do you want to tell? What life message do you want your life to speak of? What imprint do you want to remain when you are no longer physically here? What beginnings do you want to come from your endings?

We are opening our minds to a different relationship with loss and grieving. A relationship where, instead of dreading when love will become loss, we open ourselves to the new manifestations of love that come from loss.

Impermanence and Uncertainty

The lesson of loss is that life is bittersweet, and what we treasure most is never meant to last forever. From moment to moment, everything, even at a cellular level, is changing. When we acknowledge that the most natural and consistent thing in the world is change, our ability to value the present moment expands. Like nothing else, impermanence can teach us how to treasure every aspect of life and live wholeheartedly.

How can we look at impermanence differently, as if nothing is ever lost, only transformed? What if grief could offer us guidance on how to live?

Instead of resisting the temporary nature of things, loss can become something that makes us live in more appreciation. Leading with curiosity, we ask ourselves, *Since loss is certain, what do I value here and now? How am I showing appreciation for what I love as well as what I've lost?* Answering these questions, loss takes on a new meaning, a rousing purpose.

Making peace with loss includes surrendering to uncertainty. As humans, our brains are constantly trying to foresee what will happen next so we can prepare ourselves. We want to know what's coming. We want things to happen in our own time. We want to control the beginnings and endings. But life doesn't work that way. Discerning what we can and can't control, what we know and what we don't know, is another life lesson that comes with impermanence.

In *When Things Fall Apart: Heart Advice for Difficult Times*, Pema Chödrön says, "Letting there be room for not knowing is the most important thing of all. When there's a big disappointment, we don't know if that's the end of the story. It may just be the beginning of a great adventure. Life is like that. We don't know anything. We call something bad; we call it good. But really we just don't know."

We don't know if the relationship that just ended will create space for a healthier, more aligned connection in the future. We don't know if a health condition that we didn't choose could be the impetus for a spiritual awakening. We don't know if the rejection that sent us reeling will be the beginning of a powerful redirection. We resist because saying hello to the new means saying goodbye to what we know. But something has to end for us to take the next step in life, and I've come to believe that when something ends, there is always something just as meaningful coming our way.

When we experience a loss, whether it is by choice or not, there is more to discover beyond the resistance and fear. We also have the opportunity to develop courage and see where our stories take us next. Our creative control lies in our ability to assign meaning. We give ourselves more options when we regard loss as a part of life that nourishes the soul instead of something that depletes it. Loss gives us practice in holding life with a gentle hand, trusting the natural order of things, and focusing on the adventure.

What Do You Believe?

My brother Greg and I were born seventeen years apart. As a child, he was mostly a mystery to me. Looking through photo albums, I saw him as the tall, dark, handsome figure in the sepia-colored picture, rocking a magnificent Afro while holding me, his newborn baby sister. He was a clean-shaven soldier in the navy blue air force uniform smiling in front of a US flag. He was my sister's older brother, my dad's first child. We had different moms, and my mother did not make my brother (or my sister) feel welcome in our home, so I didn't get to truly know him as a person until I was an adult.

By the time I was old enough to have memories, he was away in the air force, then he was in culinary school, then he was here and there, out in the world, living his life. Our nana's house in the Hill District was the home base of my dad's side of the family, and that is where my brother and I bonded. I moved there in 1996 when my mother moved to New York and my childhood home was foreclosed. I was in college, and he was in and out of town, but every time we saw each other, we picked up where we left off and learned more about each other.

Our family tradition when all the siblings and cousins were home visiting was to eat dinner together around the table, then curl up and watch movies and have dessert. I can still hear the voices—echoes of storytelling, teasing, laughing, and arguing. It felt like those times would never end. But from 2017 to 2021, three people from those family gatherings at Nana's have passed away—my dad, my aunt, and then my brother. Nana's house has been emptied out and sold. Time moves on, and I look through photos and cling to memories, wondering if I was grateful enough, if I was present enough. Did I realize how precious and temporary those moments were?

I didn't get to say goodbye to my brother. I didn't hear his voice or see his face for over a year before he died. So I not only mourn his death; I mourn the time I didn't spend with him when he was alive. I wish I'd reminded him more often that he was important to me. I wish I'd asked more questions about his life and that I'd made more space in mine for him. He faced more than his share of adversity, and I never told him how much I admired his generous spirit and resilience through it all.

Losing my dad, my aunt, and then my brother so close together awakened a deeper commitment to honor what is sacred in my life, now with the earned wisdom of someone who has accumulated loss. I try not to dwell for too long on the time we did not get or the regrets that I have because I know our time together has not ended; it has only transformed. The best way I know to honor my recent ancestors is to continue to learn from those relationships even though they're physically gone, to talk about them and what I learned from their lives and their deaths, and to show up in the relationships that I value with more intention and appreciation.

The great truth about life is that it is both heartwarming and heartbreaking. Whether it is heartbreak and shame over losing my relationship with my mother; grief from losing loved ones; or regret and shame over past decisions, missed opportunities, and broken friendships, I have woven these plot points into my story with my belief system as a guide to meaning. I believe that everything begins with love, exists because of love, and returns to love in the end. This is the through line in how I arrange my creative material—the beginnings, the rising action, the inciting incidents, turning points, and resolutions in my life.

What do you believe? What is your through line, and where does it come from? Your belief system may come from your religious upbringing, cultural background, or life experience. It's okay to question it. It's okay if you're uncertain. We will discuss more about beliefs in part III, but for now, be curious and recognize the role that your beliefs play in how you construct meaning after loss.

Storytelling and Nostalgia

When we lose something that we weren't ready to lose, we have the choice to remain open to love or close ourselves to avoid future hurt and loss. We need to give ourselves space to reconstruct meaning in our lives. We need to reconcile how it has changed us, how we navigate new storylines and cope with the day-to-day reality of it. We have to relearn our place in the world with our losses lovingly included and honored in our identities.

Storytelling has been the most powerful source of healing in my life. I used to think about my past and ruminate on the same losses and disappointments over and over again. But when I started writing about it, I learned to include it all. The joy and the laughter as well as the pain, shame, and regret. There's plenty I don't remember, but when I start with an object, a moment, a feeling, then gently, little by little, the detail blooms into more. Storytelling gives your memories a stage where the sweet and the bitter tell an intimate story that captures universal truths. There is more than loss in your story; there are complex characters and emotional connections that don't lose their value when they come to an end. There is sacrifice and risk and adventure that don't lose value even when they result in pain. There are comforts, pleasures, and delights that nourish us through all the endings and all the pain. The way we honor the fullness of our life experience through our stories makes us active creators in the transformation of loss.

What other creative choices do we have when it comes to loss? Immediately, nostalgia comes to mind as a source of creative inspiration and a way to bring to life what is lost. Nostalgia is this transcendent force that comes over me and carries me away to different times in my life more and more often as I get older. According to research by the University of Essex in the United Kingdom, nostalgia offers solace in the face of loss and relief in the form of love: "Nostalgia is uniquely positioned among emotions in offering a bridge from loss to love."

Nostalgia is bittersweet. It awakens appreciation for the past and brings brightness to the here and now. An old song, movie, or book can remind you of prior versions of yourself. A familiar landscape or route can remind you of a certain season of your life. Nostalgia can be a restorative visitor during times of stress and uncertainty. It can also be a rejuvenating force that keeps the spirit of what you've lost alive. Nostalgia reminds us that we can still feel the warmth of the people and times that we've lost.

When we bring nostalgia and storytelling together to reminisce with others, it promotes unity and social connectedness, which are also vital to healing. Engaging with people who are honoring their grief; comforting each other in the losses; forging new connections, beginnings, and openings shows us that, yes, love can change form. Cultivating a supportive community around yourself provides comfort and reduces feelings of loneliness. Community (which can be any size, even one or two people) is one of the most beautiful things that can come from loss because it gives birth to new beginnings. In the words often attributed to Seneca, a Roman Stoic philosopher, then brought to my ears by Semisonic, a '90s-era alternative band, "Every new beginning comes from some other beginning's end."

As the innate impulse to cling to the past fades, you will become more open to exploring resources for adapting to change when loss arrives. If we do not reframe our relationship with loss, we make it harder to receive what is yet to come. The bittersweet void that is left may never go away, but there is still room for more life, love, and connection.

Remember that grief is not here to destroy you; it is here to awaken you. Like any other emotion, it comes seeking expression. When we suppress it by ignoring it or compound it by punishing ourselves, we force grief to stay put instead of letting it move through us. When we meet grief with reverence, we can learn to ride the waves and surrender to deep appreciation, wonder, and joy at the miracle of life.

Reflection: What Grief Needs to Say

> *Everything you love will probably be lost, but in the end, love will return in another way.*
>
> —Franz Kafka

A creative approach to grief reveals the aspects of what you've lost that are still available to you. With the understanding that grief occurs in many contexts—whether it's loss of health, a loved one, a job, or anything else—we can creatively activate the essence of what we've lost through ritual, storytelling, nostalgia, and community.

Creativity has the power to transform pain into inspiration. What does grief need to say through you? The exercises below offer ways for you to explore this question:

1. **Freestyle write:** Do a brain dump to get all your emotions out and name your feelings. Identify the sensations in your body when you think about what you've lost. Be curious and open to how you feel, not judgmental. It doesn't make the pain go away, but it offers insights, promotes self-awareness, and supports the healing process.
2. **Tell yourself the story:** What grief story do you need to tell? You can write about what life was like before the loss, during, and after. You can write stories to refresh your memories. If it still hurts too much to write in the first person, you can write a fictional story to channel your emotions through characters. Creativity has the power to transform pain into inspiration.
3. **Write a letter:** What are the words that you didn't get to say? By writing a letter to the one(s) you lost, you get to safely express yourself and continue your relationship with that person in a new and evolving way.
4. **Write down your prayers:** What do you need to say to God, to life, to the universe, to whatever you call your creator or higher power? When you're hurting and disillusioned, sometimes it's easier to write it down than to say it aloud.
5. **Keep a list of lessons and silver linings:** As part of your healing journey, keep a log of insights, lessons, positive aspects, and reasons for gratitude that are being revealed to you, even as you struggle. Balance out the pain by acknowledging the love and joy that remain.

It was through freestyle writing (#1) that I admitted the guilt and regret I was feeling over the loss of my brother and the need to forgive myself. And it was through the practice of listing lessons learned (#5) that I began to recognize the beginnings of a new story, one where I grow from loss and allow the pain to fuel more conscious choices.

I will never tire of celebrating the power of words to give voice to the truest parts of ourselves. In our final section, "Voice and Vision," we will fully step into our roles as the narrators of our life stories and examine how our words, mindsets, and lifestyles give meaning to our vast experiences.

Part III

Voice and Vision

If you inherently long for something, become it first. If you want gardens, become the gardener. If you want love, embody love. If you want mental stimulation, change the conversation. If you want peace, exude calmness. If you want to fill your world with artists, begin to paint. If you want to be valued, respect your own time. If you want to live ecstatically, find the ecstasy within yourself. This is how to draw it in, day by day, inch by inch.

—Victoria Erickson

Chapter Eight

The Power of Words

"I'm so bad at math."

I made this announcement to my aunt one morning at the kitchen table during my freshman year of college. I must have been home for a holiday. I was rambling on about my classes while Aunt Mimi scrawled notes into her journal next to me; bottles of vitamins and supplements spread out in front of her on the table.

Looking up from her notes, she hissed at me, *Tssssk. Tsssk. Tsk!* A verbal smack on the hand to interrupt my complaint. She reached out to my chin to turn my face to hers.

Peering over her reading glasses, she looked into my eyes and scolded, "Don't limit yourself that way." Then she turned her attention back to her vitamins and her studies.

"What way? It's a fact. I'm *not* good at math."

Without looking up, she said, "Why do you say that?"

"Because math is hard! It doesn't come naturally to me like words do."

"So is it that you aren't good at math, or is it that math is hard?"

I stared at her, genuinely confused at this point. "Same thing, isn't it?"

Shaking her head, she said, "Noooo. No. Not at all. You're basically saying that anything that's hard for you, you're not good at."

She looked up to meet my eyes again before continuing.

"Thinking that way will keep you from trying things that might be hard at first but are good for you. Don't sell yourself short. You could say, '*I have to work hard at math.*' But don't say you're not good at math. Then you're just shutting yourself down."

Aunt Mimi was known for bright colors and eccentric habits, for dancing between silly and serious, laughing and scolding. She was my dad's younger sister, a Scorpio, her birthday two days before mine in November. I was scared of her as a child because she wouldn't let me get up from the table until I'd eaten everything on my plate, and I had to use my whole voice around her—not the soft, timid one—because she didn't cater to my shyness.

She was the kind of person who made all her meals from scratch and didn't believe in traditional medicines. She studied holistic wellness and kept logs of all the vitamins and nutrients she was taking. A massage therapist by trade and a mixed-media artist by craft, she had no kids of her own but had close relationships with her twelve nieces and nephews. When I was in my twenties, she was in her sixties, and she took on the role of a guide in my story—like we talked about in chapter 6—sharing as much wisdom and knowledge with me as I was willing to receive. We bonded over our shared interest in spirituality, creativity, and well-being. She taught me that the words I use to talk about myself matter.

At the time, I heard her, but I didn't *hear* her. *Adults are so dramatic*, I thought. *They're just words!* As a college student, I was still under the trance of fitting in—talking how my peers talked and thinking how I'd been programmed to think. Self-deprecation was a way to manage expectations and not get anyone's hopes up, especially my own. I didn't think that a simple matter of word choice could be that serious or make a difference in how I fared in class. I had no problem with math in school until I had to take calculus during my freshman year of college; then it became an issue. I practiced and studied and was barely able to pass. The struggle stirred up limiting stories that I'd accepted as truth over the years: *I should get it right the first time. I shouldn't be confused. I shouldn't have to ask for help.*

Being a good student was my claim to fame as I graduated from high school with a merit-based scholarship and a four-year internship all lined up. But there was a certain resilience I didn't learn in high school that I would need in order to be successful in college and beyond. I didn't know how it felt to study and still struggle, how to fail and keep trying. I didn't know how to receive constructive criticism without getting defensive. I didn't know that the quality of my life would be affected by my ability to nurture a state of mind where my thoughts didn't work against me when I was facing hard things. It didn't click for me that day in the kitchen, but my curiosity was piqued.

Reclaiming Our Thoughts

Our words carry creative energy. The words *I am* are powerful, and we need to be mindful of how we complete them because when we do, we are defining ourselves. What we say we are becomes our reality as we subconsciously create experiences that confirm what we believe.

So far while reflecting on the origins of our defeated storylines and limiting beliefs, we've peeled back layers to face truths, assumptions, and fears that have shaped our paths. It is a radical thing to open our minds and accept that we have the power to change our stories. An unexpected challenge that comes with this enlightenment is grasping what it calls for day to day in terms of self-talk and how we express ourselves.

It's easy to overlook this part of the transformation, where we observe our daily habits and rhythms to see how our thought patterns and lifestyles either support or take away from the new stories we are crafting. We must study the building blocks, our habits of thought, because they affect how our stories unfold. Our words have the power to elevate us or hurt us, and we can harness this power when we are intentional with our language.

What do your everyday thoughts reflect about your relationship with yourself? Are you beating yourself up every time you make a mistake? Are you complaining, blaming, and pointing fingers? Are you talking yourself out of opportunities? Are you imagining worst-case scenarios?

Our thoughts come from mental activity in our brains that is shaped by our experiences and environments, families and friends, teachers and peers, and all the news, media, movies, and TV that we consume. The subject of reclaiming our thoughts may be a touchy one for those of us who experience intrusive thoughts, which can be brought on by stress or can be an ongoing symptom of anxiety, depression, or other mental health conditions. Intrusive thoughts are unwanted and uninvited ideas and images that come into our minds without warning. If you know like I know, they can fall on the spectrum of annoying to downright disturbing, causing you to worry, feel shame, or numb yourself with vices to escape them. Intrusive thoughts can be violent, tragic, mean, or even creepy. What makes them intrusive is that they do not reflect our morals and intentions; they reflect our stress and trauma. When we understand that, we can free them to pass through our minds without clinging to them.

When I became a mom at the age of twenty-three disturbing images of something terrible happening to my baby would pop into my head. I didn't know anything about postpartum anxiety at the time, so I was ashamed and didn't tell anyone. Twenty-two years later, I still experience intrusive thoughts daily. Sometimes it's when I'm in the grocery store or at a mall, and I have a disturbing thought about a shooter coming in or the building blowing up. I'll be riding down the highway and thinking that one of my tires is going to blow out, making me lose control of the car. Sometimes it's when I'm doing nothing at all, and a train of thought turns dark, and all of a sudden I'm thinking about every mistake I've ever made, every person I've hurt, and that familiar voice inside telling me that I'm a bad person. Sometimes I spiral for a while before I catch myself, but it doesn't go as far. The difference now is that I have coping techniques, and I will share some of them with you in a moment. Eventually, I label the unwanted visitor as an intrusive thought and let it go. We can label and let go of any thought we don't want to give energy to when we know that we are not our thoughts. Our arbitrary ideations do not define us.

It is repetition that generates a creative charge, turning thoughts and ideas into beliefs, attitudes, and ongoing inner narratives. It is action that gives that creative charge momentum, turning inner narratives into behaviors that shape our sense of self. This is why we take the time to observe our thoughts and identify the stories we are telling ourselves. Some of our beliefs and attitudes come from seeds of thought that are buried so deep in our subconscious mind that we don't realize how much they are echoing through our actions and reactions. This hidden-away place is where my ideas about math were conceived: *I'm bad at math because I'm not smart enough. No matter how hard I study, I don't have what it takes.*

At the same time, I told myself that I could make up for my statistical limitations by being impressive in other ways: *I excel in classes that have to do with people and words. If I stay in my lane and focus on what I'm good at, I can make up for what I'm lacking.*

I thought I was being realistic and having a positive attitude about the whole thing, but there was still an energy of limitation and lack in that approach. I was giving myself permission to avoid the discomfort, succumbing to the fear of trying and failing. There was a lesson to be learned here, and my aunt was trying to poke holes in my skepticism to teach me. It would take more than one conversation to unravel the habits of thought that had systematically distorted my perception of my abilities.

Cognitive distortions are biased thoughts that interfere with a person's self-concept, how they view their daily interactions and situations, their relationships and pursuits. According to the American Psychological Association, the brain creates mental filters as shortcuts to reduce the work of processing so much information at once. This energy-saving function can also cause the oversimplification of complex thoughts, hindering our imaginations and narrowing our outlook. A few of these cognitive distortions may sound familiar.

Do you think that if something is not done perfectly, it's a waste of time or not worth doing at all? Do you automatically jump to extremes—either right or wrong, good or bad—with no middle ground? Being hypercritical and not allowing yourself to be a beginner or make a mistake is a sign that you may be a perfectionist. Perfectionism is a form of polarizing, a cognitive distortion that is characterized by an all-or-nothing mindset that is at odds with the complexity of most people's lived experiences: *If I don't get straight As, I am a failure. If this book does not become a bestseller, then I have wasted my time. If I can't guarantee success, then I'm not going to try.*

Do you find yourself fixating on your mistakes and shortcomings, unable to recognize your strengths? Are you dismissive of your positive attributes and qualities? This is called minimizing: *I know they gave me the promotion at work because I've been working there so long and they had to, not because I'm good at my job.*

Do you ever take a small piece of information and predict something that will happen based on little or no real evidence? This is called fortune-telling. Catastrophizing is a form of fortune-telling when we predict the worst possible outcome: *My partner came home late from work, so they must be cheating on me. My child is not answering their phone, so something must be wrong. I feel nervous about getting on stage, so that means I'm going to embarrass myself.*

Do you study body language, tone of voice, and behaviors and jump to conclusions, often assuming that people are thinking something negative about you? Mind reading leads to misinterpretations and judgments as we react to attitudes that may not even exist: *My neighbor didn't wave back when I saw her at the festival, so she must not like me. My coworkers didn't leave room for me at the table, so they must not have wanted me to sit with them.*

Do you often take the responsibility for other people's moods, attitudes, or circumstances? When you gratuitously blame yourself for situations that are not within your control, this is called personalizing: *My best friend didn't text me back, so she must be mad at me. I want to go by my in-laws for the holiday, but I know my parents will be disappointed, and I will be responsible for ruining their holiday.*

I've known all of these mental shortcuts far too well. In most cases, they would seem to happen automatically even before I realized what I was thinking and how I was reacting to what I was thinking. To break out of these limited stories, we need new language, starting with how we talk to ourselves. On the journey to becoming the truth teller and cycle breaker I was called to be, I had to learn how to think and talk like an intentional creator, like my words were shaping my experience—because they were.

Believing Our Thoughts

Belief is the core of creation. You can't create a piece of art, a new story, or anything without belief. So when we believe our negative thoughts, what are we creating? We are creating a world where our limiting beliefs and fatal flaws are realities, and our callings and desires are out of reach. If you believe that you are too old, too young, too slow, too fast, too weird, too broken, too sensitive, too anything, then those are lenses that you will see everything through, and those will be limitations that you have placed on yourself. The thoughts we repeatedly think become beliefs that affect our choices and how we express ourselves verbally, physically, and energetically. The words we use do matter. We are not just communicating with each other; we are also communicating with the creative power of life itself.

For most of my life, I believed all of my thoughts, that my worries were valid, true, and all equally rational and inevitable. There was no separation—my assumptions were facts, and my thoughts were reality, and they allowed me to protect myself from pain, predict outcomes, and make sense of the world as I knew it. Despite Aunt Mimi's guidance, thoughts like these played like a soundtrack in my mind over the years, reflecting the victim mentality that ordered my steps: *People don't really like me; they tolerate me. If I don't settle for this situation that doesn't feel quite right, something better may never come along. If I make a mistake, I will lose credibility. If I change my mind about something, I'm a quitter. If I decide to rest, then I'm lazy. Even if I am successful, I don't have what it takes to sustain it. I always let myself and others down.*

In *Loving What Is: Four Questions That Can Change Your Life*, Byron Katie guides the reader to question their fears and beliefs, by asking if they absolutely know if their negative beliefs are true. We addressed this earlier in chapter 2 when we asked ourselves, *What else could be true?* This is where our opportunity to create comes into play. We can use our thoughts to build a case for hope instead of despair. You might be thinking, *But I can't control my thoughts. The more I try, the more impossible it seems.* That's okay because mind control is not what this reclamation is about. The rest of this chapter is about how to change your relationship with your thoughts through mindfulness, observing them to discover which ones drain you and which ones energize you, which ones you want to align your actions with and which ones you want to dismiss.

Aunt Mimi told me that when you think new thoughts, life shows you new things, but she didn't explain the mechanics of it, the how, and the science of it. Over the years, I would seek the knowledge to connect those dots.

The Science behind the Words

Neuroplasticity is the brain's ability to restructure itself in response to functional changes from illness or injury or due to structural changes such as learning or emotional healing. We are able to learn, unlearn, and adapt throughout our lives because of this function. Neural pathways are the connections that form between neurons in the brain, and these connections represent our thought patterns.

Thinking positively charged (optimistic and hopeful) thoughts is how we disengage painful, repetitive pathways and generate new ones. The language we repeat through the thoughts we think and the words we use literally has the power to change our brains. Many of our old pathways are blanketed with negatively charged (pessimistic and hopeless) language. When we use negatively charged language, it inhibits the release of the neurochemicals like dopamine, adrenaline, and noradrenaline that manage stress, causing fear, anxiety, and distorted reasoning to increase.

When we use positively charged language, we strengthen frontal lobe activity in the brain, which is responsible for cognitive reasoning. When this happens, it allows us to break down information into manageable parts, promoting more flexible, solution-based thinking. Thoughts with a positive charge instigate healthy decisions and behaviors, while the negative, limiting ones have a demoralizing effect, preventing us from rallying to meet our challenges with willingness and courage.

According to Dr. Rick Hanson, a psychologist at UC Berkeley and the author of *Hardwiring Happiness*, repetition empowers the brain to automatically direct itself to the language it is most familiar with in any situation. This is because when we repeat thought patterns over and over again, we strengthen those neural pathways in our brains. He says that by choosing positive words and language structure more often, we can pave new pathways and discover new default reactions that strengthen us. On the other hand, this also means that repetition upholds negative language habits that can lead to long-term physical and mental burdens.

Does this mean we should be trying to control our thoughts? That if we push down our negative thoughts enough, they will be forever silenced? It doesn't work that way. Declaring "*Good vibes only!* and suppressing hurt, worried, jealous, or any kind of disheartened thoughts is a way of bypassing how you truly feel to avoid dealing with it. Toxic positivity is when we misuse optimism as an excuse to ignore negative emotions and experiences. But energy doesn't lie. Our nervous systems aren't fooled. While we don't want to reinforce negative thought loops, we do need to acknowledge what our emotions are communicating to us. We need to sit with our painful thoughts and feelings before we overwrite them with healing narratives.

Sitting with unwanted thoughts is uncomfortable, but if we get curious about them, we can become receptive to the underlying messages they have for us. If we don't let ourselves feel the discomfort, we miss the opportunity to learn something that deepens our sense of self and improves our overall well-being.

We all suppress our thoughts and emotions sometimes to get through the conversation, the situation, the day. But sometimes this avoidance can turn into weeks, months, and years, and all the things we don't face just build up. We seek relief, looking everywhere but inside. We think we can change people and circumstances around us to feel better, but all we can really control is our mental hygiene, how we witness our emotions and translate our experiences.

Our minds can be scary places. Full of doors we don't open. Voices we don't want to hear. Whether your habit is to avoid your negative thoughts and pretend they're not there or believe all of them and spiral into dark places, there are coping tools that can help you face your thoughts without being consumed by them. I wonder if you feel the same hope I do in knowing that we can change the pathways and patterns in our minds. I'm not saying that it's easy or quick, but it's possible through consistent practice and a desire to heal.

I didn't know anything about neuroplasticity when I started changing my relationship with my thoughts, but I knew that my thinking habits were a source of distress. In my twenties, if I wasn't waiting for my thoughts to become cloudy with schizophrenic delusion, then I was numbing myself to cope with existential dread, or I was battling the limiting beliefs that told me I would always fall short. My desire for peace of mind led me to read books like *Lessons in Living* by Susan L. Taylor and *In the Meantime* by Iyanla Vanzant. Their voices joined the ongoing insights from my aunt, who continued to be a guide and a sounding board, introducing me to new ways of being.

Believing New Thoughts

"You can have whatever you believe you can have. What you believe you are worthy of will be attracted to you. It's all energy."

Aunt Mimi is sitting at the kitchen table as I stand behind her greasing and twisting her silver strands, the smell of lavender shea butter in the air.

"What does that *mean* though? So you're saying that if I believe I am worthy of a million dollars, it will just show up?"

Behind her back, I roll my eyes as I finish the current twist, wrapping the ends of her hair between my index finger and thumb. I grab the rattail comb from the table to carve out the next square in her scalp.

"Child! *Listen* to what I'm saying," she says, swinging her hands like a choir director to emphasize each syllable. I can't part the next square with her head swinging around, so I gently place my hands on her shoulders to still her.

As I continue with the next section of hair, she tells me about positive affirmations—phrases or statements used to replace unhelpful thoughts with empowering ones. She says we can use affirmations as a tool to speak our desires into existence.

I didn't understand this woo-woo stuff she was talking about, but the concept captivated me. I sensed there was something sacred at the center of it, a message for me from the universe. Still, attaching the word *worthy* to myself didn't feel right. Growing up with my mother—whose religious delusions often drowned out the enlightened spiritual teachings she gave me—it had been instilled in me that I was inherently devious and wrong, an instrument of the invisible forces that sought to persecute her. At church, I was taught to direct all positive affirmations—in other words, praise—to God in heaven. I was taught that I was decidedly not worthy, born in sin, a victim of the flesh. What Aunt Mimi was saying went against all of this, and yet it sparked hope. I was still on my way to defining my own spirituality, but I was open to the idea that I could be worthy, at the very least, of being rescued from the defeat that dominated my thoughts.

Aunt Mimi told me that writing and speaking affirmations tune your mind to the frequency of how you want to feel and be, reprogramming negative thoughts. Years later, I would read about the power of positive affirmations in *The Secret* by Rhonda Byrne and *You Can Heal Your Life* by Louise Hay. I tried writing my own, customizing them to my needs. I repeated them in my head while meditating or anytime I was trying to chase away negative thoughts. I recited them while looking at myself in the mirror. I found guided meditations where a voice chanted positive mantras. Eventually, I sprinkled the affirmations everywhere—throughout my journals, on post-it notes on mirrors, as screensavers on my phone—hoping the high-vibe words would become second nature: *I am whole. I am worthy. I am safe.*

The problem was that I didn't feel anywhere close to whole, worthy, or safe, and deep down I still didn't believe these things were possible for me. Affirmations gave me license to state the things I wanted to believe, and many of them were treasured reminders that I embraced without resistance. But what I couldn't shake through writing, reciting, and listening to affirmations was the awareness that some of them were simply unbelievable to me.

I started referring to these elusive affirmations as aspirational beliefs. These are ideals that we want to embody, but we have doubts that undermine them. Our aspirational beliefs stem from our values, principles, and authentic needs. Meanwhile, our doubts stem from our limiting beliefs, which often express themselves through the voice of our inner critics.

No matter how many times I repeated my aspirational beliefs, my tragedy story was still the dominant narrative in my mind when I dared to admit my most heartfelt desires. I didn't have it in me yet to truly believe that I could feel whole, worthy, and safe in my story. I would often look back at my personal history, where mistakes and disappointments were pieces of evidence building a case against me, proving my guilt and unworthiness. And I couldn't fathom my life ever being another way. Stubbornly, the hope remained, and a tug-of-war ensued: my heart full of belief, my mind full of doubt.

When my heart said, *Everyone is unique and creative in their own way, and our purpose as humans is to be true to ourselves,* my mind said, *Except for you. If you reveal who you really are, you will be judged, criticized, and rejected, and no one will understand you.* When my heart said, *I believe in my gifts and talents, and I have what it takes to use them successfully*, my mind said, *You're not good enough, smart enough, or disciplined enough to show up consistently, and you've proven that time and again.*

I figured that with persistence, my mind would catch up to my heart, and my doubts would fade. I continued to read inspirational books and write affirmations, but the disconnect remained. I knew that if I truly wanted to align with my aspirational beliefs, I would have to find a way to create affirmations that would teach my mind to work in service of my heart instead of my fears. Once again, I turned to mindfulness, a useful tool for paying attention without judgment in any realm, particularly when it comes to observing our habits of thought.

Thought Labeling

Being Zen by Ezra Bayda introduced me to a concept called *thought labeling*, a mindfulness practice that I applied to both journaling and meditation. According to Bayda, thought labeling helps us see what we are thinking, giving us a way to escape our mental loops. The instruction is that when thoughts arise, you label them and let them go. Here is how I applied that guidance.

When I journaled, I set a timer and transcribed my mental chatter in a stream-of-consciousness fashion. Then I would come back later, read my journal entries, and notice patterns. For example, if I wrote, *I am overwhelmed from taking care of everyone else before myself, but if I stop, I will disappoint people, and they will think I'm selfish*, I might label this as *having a thought that it's selfish to take care of myself first*, or *I see myself believing that I must please others before taking care of myself*, or *worrying about what others think*, or *people-pleasing*.

In this example, I observed how my habitual thoughts and worries about pleasing other people were in conflict with my authentic needs and boundaries. You could also label a thought by stating the name of the person who implanted it in your mind. Naming helps you notice when your thoughts come from other people's words and opinions.

When I meditated, I applied the thought-labeling concept by visualizing my thoughts passing by in my mind like clouds in the sky. I practiced labeling them without judging them. For example, if my stream of consciousness sounded like *I need to fit in a workout today, but if I don't get these reports done, I will fall behind and have to ask for more time, and everyone will know that I'm really a fraud and can't handle the responsibility,* I might label this as *attaching my worth to productivity,* or *focusing on scarcity,* or *catastrophizing.*

Labeling your thoughts and feelings without self-judgment interrupts the familiar pattern and allows you to distance yourself and move on without clinging to the passing illusion. After these sessions, I would reflect on the patterns I noticed and the meaning I could extract from them. In this example, I noticed how frequently I worried about getting things done and how much I attached my sense of well-being and self-worth to my productivity. I also noticed how mechanical it was for me to take a thought and spin it into a whole story full of assumptions.

These practices provided me with a purposeful way to sit with my thoughts and feelings and examine them. The more you become a witness to your thoughts, the more the way you process them changes. It becomes easier to dismiss the ones that undermine you. This is the difference between bypassing our thoughts *without* reflection and acknowledging our thoughts *with* reflection—we sit with the thoughts long enough to see what messages they carry and what feelings and stories are attached to them.

When I started doing this, I was surprised by the vast spectrum of my thoughts and how much they contradicted each other. I saw the inner conflicts—dreaming of the best but assuming the worst. I saw the multiple identities—the easygoing good girl and the rebellious free spirit. I saw the push and pull between ambition and anxiety, courage and fear.

What do you think you would notice if you observed your thoughts this way? Mindfulness primes us to sort through all the noise in our heads and discover what centers us, what holds us together, as well as what distracts us from our values and the truth of who we are. Through mindful observation, I became consciously aware of the themes that I was perpetually thinking, writing, and talking about. As I wrote and reflected on what I wrote, I began to distinguish between the voice of my higher self and the voice of my fears.

Thought labeling also made me more aware of my conversational patterns. As someone who craves soulful connections with other people, my version of small talk includes revealing what moves you, what keeps you up at night, what makes you who you are. I would say things like "*I'm so bad at math*," or "*There are no good jobs anymore*," or "*I'll be happy when I finally pay off all this debt*" as a way of offering up my fears and wobbles to elicit an honest conversation about the hard things in life or something real under the surface. This was my way of being vulnerable and making sincere connections. But I began to notice that this approach usually resulted in me complaining and carrying on about my limitations and doubts. How hard things are. How little I have. How much I'm dreading this or that because something always goes wrong.

My coworker might say, "*Congratulations on the new job!*" My response would be, "*Thanks, but it's really not a big deal. I will basically be doing the same thing as before but more of it. I know it's going to be overwhelming, and I'm already stressed.*" At a social gathering, one of my friends might say to someone,

"My friend GG here writes books. She has self-published two already, and they're really good. You should check them out." My response would be, *"Oh yeah, they're just about my feelings and stuff, if you're into that. I did everything myself, so they are pretty amateur, but, you know, you can get them on Amazon."* What a sales pitch, right? I started asking myself, *Why do I always sound so defeated?* I realized this narrative wasn't keeping it real; it was keeping me low and depleting my energy.

The investigation didn't stop there. I also noticed how heavy it felt to gossip about people and make judgments about their lives. Comparing, criticizing, and complaining are mind-closing, heartbreaking habits that drain our creative energy, but they are ingrained in our culture, in the way we talk and interact with each other. As an artist who values the freedom to make creative choices and express myself wholeheartedly, I care about giving others the same space that I want for myself. For instance, if I believe in compassion and nonjudgment, but in my mind and in my conversations I'm comparing and criticizing myself and others, that contradiction won't feel good in my spirit. So I had to take an honest look at my narratives and begin to unlearn these societal habits.

When I stopped voicing fears, complaints, and judgments as a way to connect with others, I found the courage to communicate in more meaningful ways. Conversations that were about ideas and possibilities and meaning. Exchanges that left me uplifted and wanting to take inspired actions. People who match that energy will gravitate toward you when you speak from this higher vibration. I was making these discoveries while living my life, raising my kids, and navigating relationships and social environments—treating myself like my own test subject.

Because I'd been at the mercy of my doubts, fears, and negative thoughts for so long, I knew that I needed tools to facilitate change and that writing would play a key role in this transformation. I remembered what Aunt Mimi taught me about reframing unhelpful thoughts with affirmations, and I thought, *How else can I use writing to create new pathways in my mind? What if I wrote affirmations that incorporated the voice of my higher self along with the voice of my doubts in an empowering and actionable way?*

Actionable Values

We are first introduced to values through our families of origin, religion, culture, and society. However, as we grow in our individuality, we come to recognize the intrinsic values that we can only discover through our personal experiences, principles, and passions. There comes a time when we must separate what is ours and what is not, recognizing the values that come from our lived experience and those that have been imposed on us. Our values are the qualities, ideals, and characteristics that we exude when our words and actions align with our authenticity.

Values are the foundation of our aspirational beliefs, the intentions of our higher selves. You feel them in your heart; you seek them in your mind. When we are bewitched by doubt and lose our way, our values provide a glowing path back home. Values are the tiebreakers when our minds say no and our hearts say yes, when our limiting beliefs say we can't and our aspirational beliefs say we can. So how do we affirm our values and bring them to life in our thoughts, beliefs, and behaviors?

We make them actionable. Actionable value statements were my response to the problem I faced with affirmations. I transformed my aspirational beliefs into actionable values by translating them into aligned decisions and behaviors. Here is an example:

Aspirational belief (affirmation): *I am whole. I am worthy. I am safe.*

Limiting belief (doubt): *Most of the time, I feel broken, inadequate, and bruised. When I tell myself that I am worthy, my mind reminds me of all the ways I fall short. I never feel safe.*

Then I ask myself: What are my values when it comes to this contradiction? What values do I want my life and decisions to reflect? In this example, the first thing that comes to mind is faith. I want to be fueled by faith, not fear. I also think about creativity. No matter what my mind says, I want to choose flexibility and imagine new pathways. So which actions and practices bring these values to life?

Actionable value statement: *I am whole. I am worthy. I am safe. Spiritual practice through prayer, meditation, and writing deepens my capacity to find peace and value in the present moment instead of drifting into regrets from the past and worries about the future.*

So now I have an affirmation, supported by an actionable value statement, that I can boldly recite and wholeheartedly manifest because it includes an aligned action that carries me from fear to faith. This method is ideal for those affirmations that your mind rejects, a bridge that carries you from your current mindset to the embodiment of your aspirational belief. We can build bridges like this anytime we reach the edge of our comfort zones.

It's All Connected

Imagine you are writing a fictional story. You are creating characters, relationships, settings, and situations—you are building a whole world. One of the first things you will ask yourself is: *What do my characters want?* Then you might ask yourself: *What do my characters believe?* Your answers to these questions will drive the behavior of your characters and the plot of the story, as need, desire, and circumstance collide to create the rise and fall of a narrative arc.

As you contemplate what you want to happen in your story, you will ask yourself more questions: *What are my characters thinking, fearing, and craving? What wounds do they have, and what do they need to overcome?* You will keep these things in mind as you map out their journey—where they go, what they see, who they meet, and how it changes them. You will have an intimate relationship with your characters' thoughts when they say what they say and do what they do to move the story along. You will think about cause and effect as you dream up their adventures, carefully crafting each dialogue and scene to illustrate how the characters' beliefs and desires induce their actions.

It is possible to apply this level of creativity and intention to your real-life story. You can become intimately aware of how your thoughts, beliefs, and actions affect your fate. Unlike your fictional story, you can't orchestrate other people and the world around you. You can't control the family or country you are born into. You can't control accidents, illnesses, and natural disasters. You can't control people's opinions about you. But you *do* have creative control over how you respond to the uncontrollable. You can be discerning about the habits you cultivate to deal with life's uncertainties. You can choose how you cope with intrusive thoughts. You can choose how you interact with a coworker who rubs you the wrong way. You can choose how you respond to people who have different backgrounds and beliefs than you. When you are reactive, you are making decisions from your wounds and fears, making choices you don't even realize you are making. Using self-discovery tools, you can observe your thoughts and feelings and make value-based decisions, making you an intentional creator instead of a reactive one.

Changing your relationship with your thoughts is a fundamental part of your healing journey. The words you choose are narrating your story, and they do make a difference. It all connects back to finding wisdom in your experiences and using that wisdom to construct the path ahead. I think back to the silence that hovered over my childhood and how finding my voice and cultivating new language changed my life. It's become a mission in my life to liberate the words that were caught in my throat and help others do the same. I've built a community and business around words and breaking silences through writing. I found value-based reasons to speak up, and my reasons gave me courage where there used to be none.

If your thoughts have been a source of distress and disconnection, you can build new pathways that help you respond to old feelings in new ways. You can elevate your awareness and learn to cultivate thoughts that turn into inspired words and actions. This is how we reclaim our stories. The inner work we do as individuals serves a universal purpose. Even if you don't share your story in a public way, the way you live your life tells a story that ripples into the lives you touch. The paths you choose and the bridges you build give others insight into your values.

I carried my aunt's teachings with me through life. She gave me the awareness to look at my thoughts differently, and in doing so, she contributed to generational healing that I can also pass along to my descendants. Together we can challenge the societal norms that perpetuate negative thought patterns that keep us small, divided, and disempowered.

Reflection: Actionable Values

Words are singularly the most powerful force available to humanity. We can choose to use this force constructively with words of encouragement, or destructively using words of despair. Words have energy and power with the ability to help, to heal, to hinder, to hurt, to harm, to humiliate and to humble.

—Yehuda Berg

You can't believe everything you think. We tell ourselves stories through our thoughts. Unexamined thoughts create a limited story about who you are, what you can and can't do, and who you can be. We shouldn't underestimate the power of the words we think, say, and absorb. They carry an energy that can buoy us or bring us down. If we understood the power of our words, we would use them to build, not destroy. We would align our words with our creative visions and use our voices to speak for what we believe in.

We can change the momentum of our lives by changing the manner in which we talk to ourselves and the conversations we entertain. Mindfulness offers creative ways to observe your feelings and actively choose the thoughts you want to give energy to and the ones you want to release. Be patient because changing your thoughts will take consistent, dedicated practice. You will notice times when your thoughts and words contradict your truths and values. Through story work, you have tools to trace back to the origins of those inner conflicts so you can get to the heart of your aspirational beliefs and build your story from an authentic place.

In this exercise, you will complete a series of phrases that invite you to free your voice, declare the truths you want to live by and what values you want to be a voice for. As you do this, you are also identifying aspirational beliefs and the limiting beliefs that undermine them. You will then create an actionable value statement to support you in carving out new neural pathways that lead to new stories.

- Aspirational belief (affirmation):
  I want to believe . . .

  Limiting belief:
  But my doubts say . . .

Actionable value statement:
When I do (insert empowering habit or practice), *I overcome* (insert limiting belief), *and I make* (insert aspirational belief) *possible.*

- Aspirational belief (affirmation):
  I want to be a voice for . . .

  Limiting belief:
  But my doubts say . . .

  Actionable value statement:
  When I do (insert empowering habit or practice), *I overcome* (insert limiting belief), *and I make* (insert aspirational belief) *possible.*

- Aspirational belief (affirmation):
  I am breaking away from . . .

  Limiting belief:
  But my doubts say . . .

  Actionable value statement:
  When I do (insert empowering habit or practice), *I overcome* (insert limiting belief), *and I make* (insert aspirational belief) *possible.*

- Aspirational belief (affirmation):
  I am calling in / claiming / inviting in . . .

  Limiting belief:
  But my doubts say . . .

  Actionable value statement:
  When I do (insert empowering habit or practice), *I overcome* (insert limiting belief), *and I make* (insert aspirational belief) *possible.*

- Aspirational belief (affirmation):
  I want to explore . . .

  Limiting belief:
  But my doubts say . . .

  Actionable value statement:
  When I do (insert empowering habit or practice), *I overcome* (insert limiting belief), *and I make* (insert aspirational belief) *possible.*

When our thoughts improve, our well-being improves, so if we want to change how we think, we also need to change how we live. Just as we need to observe our thoughts and the things we say to understand how they are affecting our stories, we also need to give this same focus to our habits and how we spend our time. In the next chapter, we will turn to the creative process of self-care to ensure that our daily practices support our well-being and the stories we want to set in motion.

Chapter Nine

Life as a Creative Process

On a chilly day in early 2018, a few months after my dad died, I walked out of the hospital and stopped on the sidewalk to take a deep breath. I hadn't zipped up my coat or wrapped my scarf around my neck before stepping out into the winter air, so eager was I to get out of that building and on with my day. I squinted at the sun as a cold breeze wrapped its hand around my neck, sending goosebumps down my back. Usually, I'm someone who runs from the slightest chill, but I stood still for a moment, welcoming the sensation as proof of life.

A couple of hours earlier, after walking into the hospital for my first-ever mammogram, I was prayed up and confident. Everything would be fine. The examination was precipitated by the discovery of a suspicious area in my right breast that I mentioned to my primary care doctor. She told me not to jump to conclusions, but it would be best to get it checked out. At forty years old, it was time for my first screening anyway. On the day of the examination, after being called back to the X-ray room more than once for more photos, the technician told me I would need to wait a little longer to also get an ultrasound. My confidence wavered as I watched several women come in after me and leave before me. I sat in the waiting room by myself, wondering if my life was about to change and how to feel.

At the time, my dad had just died, and I hadn't been in touch with my mother for years. Even as a grown woman, not having my parents in my life made me feel untethered and vulnerable like I could be swept away at any moment. Neither of them had been a guiding presence in my life for years due to their illnesses, but it wasn't until after Dad died that I felt this profound aloneness. Loss brings us a deeper reverence for life, and his death made me look closely at my choices, acknowledging the ways I was taking my health for granted. I'd been white-knuckling my way through mental and physical health issues even though I'd seen where that could lead to. I'd been telling myself the story that one day when I earned the right to rest, I would take better care of myself. Healthy habits were for people who already had their lives together, not someone like me who was so far behind.

I saw myself as a late bloomer. Someone who didn't start getting to know who she really was until almost thirty. Who let go of a promising career and steady income to follow her passion at thirty-five. At forty, when many of my friends were senior in their jobs and no longer struggling to find their way, I was still digging out of financial holes and making ends meet. This is where I was when my dad died, and the urgency to figure everything out, create stability, and set up my family for a prosperous future was always on my mind. I could rest when I arrived at my destination. Our beliefs fuel our actions, and I believed that slowing down would mean being left behind.

My stomach growled as I waited for my name to be called again. I hadn't expected to be there for so long, plus it wasn't unusual for me to forget to eat. Thinking about the promise I whispered to my dad in his final days, I took out my phone and pulled up the notes app to get specific about how I would take better care of myself. Number one: I would take daily walks to strengthen my body and ease my mind. Number two: I would stop eating out so much and cut back on salt and sugar. Number three: I would start going to therapy again. Already I could feel the resistance building up, but I kept going.

I would find some semblance of work-life harmony. *But how?* I would have to start investigating the aches, pain, and fatigue in my body. *Where to start?* I would have to figure out how to reduce stress and set boundaries. *What does that look like?* Across the board, I would have to find the courage to reevaluate my lifestyle habits and patterns. Even with all the mindset work I'd been doing to reclaim my story, I needed to bring these conceptual changes to life in actionable ways. Making lists was one thing, but finding the resolve to follow through is something I didn't quite trust myself to do. I was never one to be consistent about prioritizing my health, taking for granted that I would always be strong and fit. And when things weren't going my way or when I was feeling emotionally drained for any reason, any fitness or self-care routine I had in play was the first thing to go.

The way I think about self-care now as I write this is so different. Now, it is a reflection of my self-worth. I value my life and my wellness, and I know that aligning my actions with my values is the way to live my best life. But it has been a long journey of change to get here. In my thirties, I found the courage to listen to my soul's calling and redirect my career, but what could change if I applied that courage to how I approached my whole life, starting with self-care? Just as I believed I was worthy of a fulfilling career, wasn't I also worthy of a healthy lifestyle?

You might not think that self-care is something you need courage for, but I will tell you why I did. To pay attention to my needs and actionably put them first, I would have to change the way I showed up for other people. How would my partner, kids, extended family, and friends respond when I started saying no when I used to say yes? *No, I can't spend that right now. No, I'm not eating that anymore. No, I don't want another drink. No, I can't hang out because I'm going to bed early tonight. No, I prefer this over that.* How would I handle the objections, the jokes, the fear of missing out?

So often we avoid making changes that we know will rearrange our lives. I needed the courage to deviate further from my old norms and make choices that would test my relationships. I would need to set boundaries, express my preferences, and protect my energy—consistently. Imagining this boundaried version of myself was almost absurd to me when I'd gone my whole life accommodating others, thinking that going with the flow made me a good person. Once again, I was afraid of change, but I found courage by zooming out and thinking about the bigger picture.

When I reached for courage, my thoughts returned to my kids. What do I want my life story to teach them? When they look back at their childhood and the example I set, what lessons for living would they find? Would they remember me working all the time, tired and distracted, rarely taking breaks or enjoying the fruits of my labor? What am I modeling for them?

Beyond that, my thoughts went to my culture and community as a Black woman. Am I being a part of the change I want to see? In my quest for accomplishment, am I continuing a legacy of overworking and undervaluing our wellness? What role did I want to play in shaping history?

My upbringing was full of hardworking, God-loving Black folks—parents, grandparents, uncles and aunts, church family, friends of family. I had abundant examples of Black love and resilience. But as I got older and more aware as an adult, I began to detect the struggles I didn't see as a child. I saw the unhealed wounds and unhappy relationships. I saw the divisions caused by arguments and power struggles. I saw the health impacts of chronic long-term stress—high blood pressure, diabetes, alcoholism, obesity, not to mention undiagnosed mental illness. I didn't understand until later that these health issues are higher in Black people than any other ethnic group because of the weathering impact of racial oppression. From historical trauma and systemic factors to direct discrimination and microaggressions, it's all part of the Black experience in America, no matter your socioeconomic status.

When I got into the workforce at twenty-two and became a mother at twenty-three, I was unprepared for how the stress builds up. The mental load of responsibility: managing a household and financial pressures, caregiving and nurturing relationships, advancing my career. There is constant decision-making, problem-solving, and conflict resolution. I was not ready for the emotional labor that would be required of me, a sensitive soul who doesn't just get wet but intensely feels the rain.

On top of the usual stressors, being Black in America is its own particular exhaustion. While I have not been directly affected by overt racism (that I know of), when something unjust happens in the Black community—close to home or around the globe—we all feel it. This is vicarious oppression. We see our family members in the faces of the men and women killed by the police. We think about our children and how to teach them to survive in a world where some people will see them as a threat and others will see them as disposable as they move through the world with the awareness that their beautiful brown skin will in some ways make their lives harder.

I wanted to hide the hard parts of life from my children. I sheltered them like parents do to make them feel safe. I understood why the adults in my childhood often had tired eyes and a drink or cigarette in their hand. I understood why they went to the altar every Sunday to lay down their cares. I didn't grow up with guidance on how to handle stress, other than to give it to God. I fell into the habit of managing stress with unhealthy vices instead of restorative habits. For most of my adulthood, I had no commitment to self-care; all I knew how to do was push through and get to the next day.

In my world, stress was this normalized thing that you can't control. You might learn in school that a healthy diet and regular exercise reduce stress, but then you go home and don't see examples of that. In fact, you hear the people you look up to and want to be accepted by saying that healthy habits are for white people. In service of maintaining your connection to your family, culture, and community, you grow up and continue certain traditions and habits even if they are unhealthy, even if you see the detrimental long-term effects.

I was on my way to the same health outcomes that had affected my parents until I saw an opportunity to bring together personal and collective healing. I knew I needed to adopt healthier habits and start new traditions, and I was not the only one. I wanted to figure out the makings of wellness, creative living, and prosperity so I could pass this on to my kids and community. To Black people like me who saw their family members eat poorly and avoid exercise because they were occupied with survival and coping. Also to women from all walks of life, who had been taught that they have to take care of everyone else before themselves. And to the community of creatives, artists, healers, and purpose-driven changemakers who were doing the work to make the world a more loving, conscious place, who were so passionate about the work that they often neglected their need for rest and self-nourishment.

This is where my heart is. This is what stirs me to action. I want us to be well. I want us to know that self-care is community care, and it starts with each of us—a responsibility to ourselves and each other to change norms for generations to come. How could I set this example if I wasn't actually living this truth for myself? I couldn't just talk about it. I needed to live it. And not just in one area of my life but across the board. I want my story to be an example of how to live an unconventional life and dance to the beat of your own drum, inspired by your culture but not just doing things because that's how they've always been done.

My musings were interrupted when finally a doctor called me into his office, thanking me for my patience. In the chair across from him, I sat on my shaking hands and crossed my ankles to keep still as he explained why they needed additional imaging tests. He said that I have dense breasts, which essentially means that it is harder to do screenings because I have more supportive tissue in my breasts than fatty tissue, the latter being easier to see through. He said to keep doing self-examinations at home, and going forward, I would continue to get screenings once a year.

When I walked out of the hospital that day with a clean bill of health, it was like a spell had been broken. I drove home to the warm haven of my family, where each step, each conversation, each meal, each kiss, each hug, every small act, every tiny, beautiful thing felt big and generous, and I was thankful to be alive.

This is my life. For all I know, this is the only one I get. And I want to start giving thanks for it by how I take care of myself.

Creative Courage

Soon after the mammogram, I started taking morning walks. At nine, I would take my youngest daughter to her elementary school a few blocks away in our little neighborhood. Instead of dropping her off and turning left to return directly home to my laptop like I used to, I would turn right and take a loop around the community. On those walks, I would listen to YouTube videos and podcasts about creativity, spirituality, and wellness—topics that stimulated my heart and mind.

It felt good to start my day by moving my body. My physicality is a source of pleasure I'd forgotten over the years as I spent more and more time in office chairs sitting still, except for my fingers typing away. I didn't realize how much I missed the liberation of movement. Getting out of my head and into a primal, grounded version of myself. Walking unburdened me and conjured gratitude, tuning me into the rhythm of my surroundings. The air gently pushing against my skin with each step, reminding me that I am moving through an atmosphere. The awkward prance of stepping around nature's odds and ends sprinkled along the path—fallen berries, animal droppings, wet leaves, muddy puddles—remnants I didn't want to bring home with me. Ducking under the low-hanging branches overhead as I lapped the residential streets. Stopping at the corner to stare up at the sky and fill my throat, chest, and belly with air, then closing my eyes to revel in the relief of the exhale. Birds swooping and soaring, offering me their poetry. The sounds of the morning commute in the distance, just a few miles away from my walking sanctuary. Having these profound moments to connect to myself and the world around me, I was in awe of the difference it made.

While walking loosened my body, increased blood flow, and strengthened my heart and lungs, it also changed the quality of my thoughts. Thanks to the release of endorphins, my spirit was uplifted and hopeful after I walked. One foot in front of the other. Eyes to the left, to the right, up and down. According to the EMDR Institute, eye movements synthesize the functions of various parts of the brain to allow for improved information processing, cognitive insights, and elimination of emotional distress. Eye movement desensitization and reprocessing (EMDR) is a psychotherapy treatment discovered by Dr. Francis Shapiro that was originally designed to alleviate distress from traumatic memories and is now recognized as an efficacious treatment for PTSD, stress, anxiety, and depression symptoms. Since our eyes naturally move from left to right while walking, we can simulate EMDR while getting physical exercise. I experienced the decrease in negative emotions as stagnant thoughts about painful memories loosened up on those walks and new insights rose to the surface. Walking also supports the body in rewiring neural pathways, promoting a state known as divergent thinking, which allows us to generate a multitude of ideas and new perspectives. You may have heard this referred to as a state of flow, a heightened level of fluid creativity where insights and connections spontaneously download into your stream of consciousness. With each step, I seemed to be powering my vessel, generating ideas, and charging connections. Walking brought my whole body online in a way that I didn't know I was missing.

Before I started centering self-care, my creative energy was limited. I could only create or make decisions when I had an aha moment or happened to be in a certain mood. I was always looking for inspiration to land on me. I would force it with caffeine, drinking five-hour energy drinks to get my mind going, just to keep up with the idea generation I needed for my daily work as a writer and coach, plus the energy to keep up with my young kids, navigate dynamics with my partner, and be a good sister, friend, niece, cousin, neighbor, human. Walking put me in a state of flow that not only led to new ideas to pursue for writing but also for how to problem-solve and manage my household. Ideas for how to approach that difficult conversation I needed to have or how to reframe that painful memory I couldn't make peace with. Ideas for the many parts of my life became accessible through this simple practice of generative movement.

Taking walks day after day had such a rousing impact that I asked myself what other simple pleasures, what other activities and patterns of behavior could I shape my days with that would shift my default way of being to this higher level of consciousness, creating more helpful thoughts, leading to more inspired actions and decisions.

When I was driven by the fear of failure, falling behind, and running out of time, I had tunnel vision and thought I should focus all my energy on achievement and productivity. But now I was awakening to the benefits of a holistic approach to self-care as the best fuel for an abundant life. I was awakening to the need for creativity and courage to come together, enabling me to navigate the emotional and practical aspects of the life vision I was calling in.

Creative courage is the collection of instincts, urges, and clues that woke me up to the person I wanted to be and the life I wanted to live. It's the inner voice that questioned me every time I told myself I was too far behind. It's the search party that found me every time I wandered away from the promises I made to myself. Creative courage is a life-giving energy that entered my life through questions like: *What if I followed this good feeling? What if I stopped being afraid of outgrowing my current life? What if I thought differently about discipline, routine, and habits? What if I made decisions with my needs in mind? What might I find on the other side of my resistance?*

At the 2008 Cornell University graduation ceremony, poet and civil rights activist Dr. Maya Angelou said, "Courage is the most important of all the virtues because without courage you can't practice any other virtue consistently. You can practice any virtue erratically, but nothing consistently without courage." We do need courage to practice all the other virtues, and we need it for all the callings we want to pursue. We need it to go against the status quo. We can be informed and knowledgeable, but without courage, what will drive us to act on that knowledge in a way that aligns with our values, especially in the face of inner and outer resistance? Some of us come by this courage inherently in our temperament and personality, some have it infused in us through our upbringing, and some of us recognize the need for it later in life and have to reparent ourselves to cultivate it. All of us need habits that reinforce it.

Creative courage is the ability to face your fears and show up as your fully expressed self in your life, work, and relationships. And we cultivate this ability through the power of self-care. When we coordinate our work, rest, and play with our needs, gifts, and sense of purpose, we sustain ourselves in the most ideal way as we unfold the unique vision of the life we want.

Even though I was historically routine-resistant and wasn't sure if I could trust myself to keep my promises, I would find out that self-care could help with that too. My distrust came from years of being driven by desperation and survival, all while operating from an undernourished vessel. I didn't have the self-awareness to know how to take care of myself before, not to mention that I didn't know I was neurodivergent or the needs that came with that. No wonder I had this long history of my visions turning out to be bigger than my capacity. Through self-care, I began to build the foundation I needed to handle the emotional labor of growth and new challenges.

Reclaiming our stories is a process of daily becoming by way of authentic creative choices, harnessing the power of our thoughts as building blocks for our day-to-day actions. The decisions we make—how we start our days, what we eat, the conversations we have, the media we consume—can be purely automatic and reactive, or they can be mindful, intentional choices fueled by self-love and the courage to do things differently. All of the reflection we've done on releasing limiting beliefs, identifying our values, and peeling back our layers now needs to be activated by congruent aligned action.

Whatever you set out to do in life, whatever new pathways you are paving, self-care helps you do it with your mind, body, and soul supported.

What Do You Need?

What influences have shaped your ideas about self-care? Think about your elders, the rituals and traditions that sustained your family through seasons of adversity and survival, expansion and growth. What did taking care look like? How was it talked about? Was it positioned as a luxury only for the privileged?

Did you grow up believing it's something that made you weak or that needed to be earned? Were you told that self-care is self-ish? Did you see your elders giving all their time, energy, and compassion to others, leaving only scraps for themselves? How did other influences in art, media, and culture affect your perspective on self-care? How does self-care show up in your life today? Answering these questions will give you an idea of the stories that shape your self-care mindset.

When I read Marya Hornbacher's memoir, *Madness: A Bipolar Life*, I saw myself in her story, struggling to make changes to my lifestyle to improve my health. She talks about ignoring her doctor's guidance and managing her condition with coping mechanisms and vices. Binge drinking. Overworking. Not sleeping. Neglecting her medication. Our familiar ways of being are so alluring and comfortable when compared to the discomfort of change. She continued to relapse and struggle until she finally surrendered to what her mind, body, and spirit needed.

I felt resistance every day as I was changing my habits to center self-care. When my phone alarm went off reminding me to stop working for the day, my inner critic would whisper that I didn't get enough done and didn't deserve to rest. My mind would lead me to familiar excuses to avoid my walking/meditating/journaling routine: *I walked yesterday; I can skip a day. I don't need to stretch today. I don't have time to cook; I can order a pizza.* Boundaries were especially hard: *Which battles do I choose? How much do I compromise? Where is the line between generosity and people-pleasing, and why does it keep moving?* But as I kept going, the resistance gave way to more inquiry. I continued asking myself: *What other areas of my life need more care? What other patterns of behavior will support me in reclaiming my energy and my power each day?*

The foundation of my practice was walking in the morning, nurturing my journaling practice with daily writing, and meditating for twenty minutes a day. Journaling was a place where I could ask myself questions, noticing the variance of my moods and how different activities made me feel. It was an excellent tool for developing a self-care strategy because it took what I was carrying around in my head and allowed me to process, plan, and discover themes and patterns.

I often journaled after walking and meditating, and the pages I wrote teemed with feelings, observations, and ideas, deepening my understanding of the cause and effect of my daily experiences. I documented what was energizing and inspiring me and what was draining and distracting me. I noted what helped me focus, how it felt when I reached the edge of my capacity, and what recharged me and filled my cup. I observed how my habits contributed to how easy or hard it was to make decisions. Then I would take those observations and experiment with different rhythms and routines.

Over time, that initial self-care list I started at the hospital expanded with strategies for every aspect of my life—physical, mental, creative, professional, social, and spiritual. I thought about my needs and values and how I could express them through each of those areas. For physical well-being, I was learning how to cook meals from scratch, but in addition to the health benefits, I was supporting my financial health and showing my children that our bodies are worthy of this kind of time and attention. I got up to date on my doctor's appointments, not only for the health benefits but also to show gratitude for my body, which fed my spiritual need for reverence. For professional well-being, I experimented with new systems to manage my finances and paperwork. The added structure turned out to also be a benefit to my mental health. For my creative well-being, I asked my inner artist what she needed and revitalized my love for books, music, and movies, which forged new, aligned social and professional connections too. I asked my introverted, neurodivergent self what she needed, and the answer was stillness, quiet, and solitude, space to withdraw from the world and daydream, which fed me in every category—reducing stress on my mind and body, allowing me to make better decisions socially and professionally and to feel more centered mentally and spiritually. This was a time of soul-searching, reconnecting to my source, and creating an ecosystem of life-affirming habits and behaviors. I was beginning to see how acting on my values instead of my fears led me to take action in ways that allowed me to operate from a more magnetic place.

By now, I was excitedly sharing my journey through my online channels and with my peers. In September 2019, as if the universe was responding to my effort, I was commissioned by Rockridge Press to write a guided journal about self-care. This was an opportunity to create a resource that souls in need could use to tune in to self-care and awaken the wellspring of creative energy inside of them, which was exactly how I felt called to serve. After setting the intention that I wanted to deepen my expertise in this area so I could provide tools for the collective, I was filled with gratitude that I was given this opportunity. I was tasked with developing dozens of exercises that would guide readers through the creative process of taking stock of their needs, focusing their intentions, and taking aligned action.

In working on myself and writing that book, I saw how walking in the creative vision you have for your life comes down to habits. I had never thought of habits as an opportunity to be creative. But with that reframe, I felt a difference in my motivation as I treated my self-care journey as an exciting, creative project I was working on. The book was just a part of it because the real creative project was my life.

The Creative Process

In *The Creative Act: A Way of Being*, Rick Rubin says, "Good habits create good art. The way we do anything is the way we do everything. Treat each choice you make, each action you take, each word you speak with skillful care. The goal is to live your life in the service of art." You may not think of yourself as an artist, but your life is your most precious creative project, and your experiences are the bits and pieces you have to work with. We are all creative beings. Life continually offers us raw materials and asks, *What will you make with what you have?*

Every artist has a spark within that calls out to be expressed. The more we take care of ourselves, the more we put ourselves in a healthy state of mind, body, and spirit for life to express itself through us.

So if good habits create good art, and we are the artists of our lives, self-care allows us to design our lives in service of our unique spark. Realizing that self-care is a solution for burnout and depletion and not an escape from it, you can develop a self-care strategy to incorporate patterns of behavior in your life that energize and nurture you while unlocking your creative flow and potential. This is how self-care fuels the creative process of our lives and the callings we pursue.

In 1926, British psychologist Graham Wallas outlined the first theory of the creative process based on years of studying inventors and other creators at work. His four-step creative process presents a model of how ideas develop. His goal was to shed light on the thought process of creativity so it could be taught and utilized for more efficiency. His book *The Art of Thought* laid the groundwork for many other scientific studies on the creative process.

Humans are wired to create. Our creations start in our minds as units of thought, seeds of ideas, which we know are the building blocks of our life stories. We don't have to be scientists or consider ourselves artists in the conventional sense to leverage Wallas's steps as a guide for how to encourage the development of the thoughts and ideas we want to fertilize. We can use it for daily problem-solving, navigating change, and designing our lives in general.

As I was working on the journal, the creative process brought order to the trial-and-error way I was developing my habits. I used Wallas's four-step model to figure out which habits to cultivate to meet my unique needs and have a full and prosperous life and business without sacrificing my well-being. I thought about each step in terms of the emotions, mindsets, and patterns of behavior that synchronize work, rest, and play to support a healthy nervous system. The steps don't necessarily play out in a linear way. They overlap each other as we explore different problems and situations. But they help us realign with our needs during those times when the path gets confusing and we need to recalibrate where we are and where we are going. As I describe the steps of the process, I will walk you through how I applied them to my self-care journey.

As you read, think about your values, needs, ideas, and interests—the topics that stimulate your heart and mind and that you want to fill your days with to realize your life vision. Think about how you approach problem-solving and how you juggle the different areas of your life. What I am presenting here is a different way to think about how you structure your time and manage your energy so that from the bottom up, you are living a story that squarely reflects your needs and values, how you want to feel, the story you want your life to tell. The exercise at the end of this chapter will give you reflection questions to think about the habits and practices that support you in activating each of these steps in your life.

The first step is preparation. In this step, you are acquiring knowledge about a problem to be solved or an idea or topic you want to explore. This step involves identifying sources of information and inspiration. You observe your inner landscape for questions and concepts that relate to the ideas that interest you, and you observe the outer world for resources, perspectives, and materials that stimulate it.

To acquire knowledge, my preparation included reading books and articles, watching videos, and having discussions about self-care and mindfulness. It included taking notes in my journal about what I was observing, what was working and what was not, what was surprising, what obstacles were surfacing. With this intention in my mind, I spent less time scrolling aimlessly, entertaining distractions, and being pulled in so many directions. We are inundated with information and propaganda each day, and we forget we have the ability to filter in more of what we want and less of what we don't want. What we focus on grows, so if you want more of something in your life, the first step is to give it your attention.

The preparation step is for being intentional about gathering inputs that energize you and water your ideas. This has benefits for us creatively, mentally, professionally, socially, and even physically because everything is connected. This step relies on mindfulness, attention, and an observant posture. You want to start your days with the intention of feeling curious, resourceful, present, and purposeful. You want to have the mindset that everything can be figured out. To be prepared for life to nourish your ideas, you walk through the world with wonder and gratitude, hungry for knowledge and wisdom, trusting your curiosity to guide you and life to inspire you. You are willing to ask questions of yourself and others and embrace vulnerability as a creative resource. Which behaviors give you these feelings and cultivate this mindset? Which activities ground you in the here and now so you don't miss the clues life is offering?

To activate this step in your life, think about how you acquire knowledge and feed your curiosity. This includes the books you read, the kinds of conversations you have, the events you attend, and the decisions you make about your time. What sources give you access to new ideas, information, and knowledge? How are you creating time and space in your life for these sources?

Our interests feed our souls and motivate our actions. When we connect our interests and our needs, we don't have to force ourselves; we can naturally cultivate habits that expand our minds and enrich our lives in whatever ways we choose. What we do with the knowledge and ideas we acquire affects the narratives we adopt, the choices we make, and the stories we craft. Being intentional here makes a world of difference to our overall health, and this is only step one.

The second step of the creative process is incubation. The ideas and information gathered in preparation simmer while our minds engage with other things. This is the part where we disconnect from the conscious effort of thinking for a while and rest our minds. Rest is the most overlooked—and in my opinion, the most productive—part of the creative process. Before you object, let me explain.

I am addicted to thinking. I find it difficult, even painful, to disconnect from my thoughts, which is why I meditate. When I was overworking and stressing the most, my thoughts were in hyperdrive, and they were quite chaotic and fearful. I rarely gave myself time to rest my mind from a problem. My kids could see the tension in my face through the furrow of my brow and the tightness of my lips as I would think, think, think, trying to come up with the fastest solution possible that would result in the least discomfort or inconvenience. This led me to make a lot of decisions that provided relief in the short term but caused problems in the long term. I didn't have faith or trust that things would happen if I didn't force them in some way. That means that while I could have been stepping away from my problems to enjoy the rest of my life, instead I was constantly distracted and stressing to figure things out.

I've learned that it doesn't have to be that way. We don't have to rely solely on our thinking minds to develop our ideas and solve our problems. Incubation is anything we do to let our minds rest. Often we think that we are stuck or uninspired when we really just need to fill our minds with inputs that make us feel inspired and intrigued (preparation) and then step away from conscious thought and let our ideas simmer (incubation).

When we are not actively trying to think, and our minds are wandering—taking a drive, doing chores, or taking a shower, for example—the default mode network (DMN) does the creative work of making connections and finding solutions. The DMN is a system of connected brain areas that come to life when we allow our thinking minds to rest. When we are daydreaming or engaging in any type of introspection, we wander into creative insights that would have been inaccessible through focused, deliberate thought.

You have probably experienced this phenomenon and thought it was a fluke or coincidence, but it is scientifically sound. At any given time, you could have dozens of ideas or problems stewing in your mind. When my elders said, "Give it to God," now I see this as a version of that. We lay our cares at the altar and give our problems to God, and answers and solutions reveal themselves to us. Connecting with nature can have a similar effect, like sitting on the beach and watching the waves or lying on your back and staring up at a star-filled sky. Letting go of your ongoing mental load to lose yourself in the big picture has a way of dissolving worries and putting things in perspective. When my elders said, "When praise goes up, blessings come down," another way to look at this is that when we show gratitude by pausing to acknowledge the beauty around us, we are gifted with abundance in all its forms.

Understanding the significance of this step, we can stop overthinking, overworking, and denying ourselves rest and start cultivating feelings of ease, presence, and trust. We can have faith we are being guided by the same source that dictates the cycles of the seasons. In the spring, we seed. In the summer, we grow. In the fall, we harvest. In the winter, we rest. The ideas that fuel our lives are part of this process too. To give ourselves space for this step, we need boundaries and cut-offs that allow us to honor when it's time to shift. We need a mindset of time abundance, the belief that time is on our side. We need habits that get us out of our heads, where we overthink and worry, and into our bodies, where we surrender and let go.

What are the lifestyle habits and activities that relax you, that get you out of your head and into your body, helping you escape your daily decisions and tasks? Which habits allow your thinking mind to go on autopilot so your creative mind can gently wander? What parts of your life do you want to show gratitude for through quality time and attention but often get neglected in service of work and productivity goals? Think about your creative hobbies like drawing, crocheting, or playing an instrument. Maybe it is making something new in the kitchen or playing with a pet or taking a road trip. You can give yourself permission to carve out time for these activities, not only because it's helping you be more productive in the long run but more importantly because you simply deserve it and by reclaiming your time, you are reclaiming your story.

I used to feel like I couldn't stop to make a healthy meal or enjoy quality time with my kids until I got enough work done. As a self-employed person, you feel there is always something you can be doing: creating, marketing, strategizing, servicing, updating, organizing, and the list goes on. Everything feels like an interruption when you are operating from the fear of lack.

If you associate rest with lack, as I did, there is a trust muscle you can build by experimenting with small personal challenges that teach you it is safe to rest. To stop overworking, I had to learn to honor my cut-offs and give attention to the other parts of my life that needed it. So if I said I would stop working at

5:00 p.m., I did, even if I was stuck on an idea and really didn't want to stop until I figured it out. I honored the boundary and took the break. And sure enough, every time I did this, I would come back with more clarity on the thing I was trying to figure out. For you, this might look like blocking time in your daily schedule (even if it is just ten minutes here, ten minutes there) to take a break from working, producing, and serving in all the ways that you do so you can take a walk, prepare a healthy snack, or simply look out the window.

When you are not actively thinking or problem-solving, you receive spontaneous insights. This is the third step, illumination. This is when a breakthrough presents itself in an aha moment, a flash of insight or clarity while you are doing something else that doesn't require analytical thought. It's not always loud or big or clear; it may be a small internal voice or an impulse arising from the deeper layers of the mind to conscious awareness. It may be the answer to a question you've been asking or the next bread crumb in a path you are following. Suddenly there is a moment of clarity and connection that seems almost magical. You get a download or a solution to a problem, and it helps you determine the next step you need to take.

When this happens, we often think that the aha moment has come out of nowhere, but it is the result of the observations and information we've been gathering (preparation) and absorbing (incubation) as we move through our days. These aha moments are evidence that the creative process is happening, and we are a part of it even when we are not aware of it. To encourage more of this, you want to feel hopeful, connected, and inspired like you are expecting life to bless you with ideas and guidance at any moment. Think about the habits that keep you in an open and receptive state. Think about where you are and what you are doing when you receive spontaneous insights.

This step is dependent on building a trusting relationship with your intuition because otherwise, when those aha moments happen, you will dismiss them. Self-doubt will get in the way of the idea that is trying to develop. What activities and practices support you in strengthening your relationship with your intuition? What helps you tune out of the external noise of the world and tune in to your inner knowing? Many of the habits that support incubation will also support illumination because resting your mind is what gives way to the aha moments. You get to experiment with creating a rhythm or sequence of habits—like my walking/meditating/journaling sequence, for example—that lead to insights that help you live life with more ease and flow. When I trust this rhythm and prioritize it along with other supportive behaviors, inspired ideas for healthy ways to enrich the different areas of my life and the realization of my goals consistently come through.

In addition to trusting your intuition, for this step you need to cultivate habits that allow you to honor the insights when they arrive. Maybe that looks like writing it down, whether that is keeping a running list or journaling about it. Maybe you record voice memos, or take a picture, or call a friend or mentor to talk about it. Honoring the insights and capturing them is like saying, "Thank you. Can I have some more?" I find that the more you take the time to honor the aha moments, document them, and act on them, the more of them you receive. Each day, due to the cumulative patterns of behavior that keep me in this flow, ideas are like currency constantly flowing toward me. My ability to receive all the abundance depends on how much I am releasing old narratives and limiting beliefs to create space for habits, rituals, and activities that put me in a receptive and open state of mind.

When we connect our observations with our insights to bring the idea to life and translate raw creativity into an executable solution, this is called verification. In this fourth step, your thoughts and ideas are distilled into art, music, plans, and other forms, where you can mold and refine them. You are taking action and integrating creativity with logic to bring your ideas to life. It does not occur by accident or mood; it requires intention, purpose, and commitment.

From 2018 to 2020, I kept ongoing notes about the habits, activities, modalities, and patterns of behavior that I was researching and experimenting with to support the various parts of my life. I cycled through preparation, incubation, and illumination many times before I started to engage in verification. When I intuitively knew I was ready to start evaluating my work and making sense of it, I laid out my notes and logs, books and article excerpts, inspiration boards—all the creative material I'd gathered—and drafted my personal self-care strategy in a way that I could follow and eventually use as a model to share with others.

The results of verification will vary from person to person depending on their callings. For some, it will look like a plan of action, an outline, or a mission statement. For others, it will look like a book, an exhibit, or a presentation. For the everyday problem-solver, the verification step may lead to a solution for how to spend more time with your loved ones, how to take a trip across the country on a limited budget, or how to contribute to a cause that you're passionate about. We need devotion for this step, a tolerance for uncertainty, and a mindset of commitment and patience as we search for the magic in the mess of our raw ideas. We also need flexibility and individuality because there is no right or wrong way to bring it all together. In verification, authenticity is the goal, not perfection. You need a long-term perspective that takes the place of the need for short-term gratification.

Sometimes your seed of an idea will bloom into something more fruitful than you ever imagined. While I'd set out to figure out what healthy habits to cultivate for a thriving creative life, the process led me to not only achieve that but to also build a comprehensive workshop experience to guide others through the process of discovering this for themselves. What came out of it was the first iteration of the Creative Courage Writing Intensive, which is the foundational framework of my creative coaching practice where participants are provided with tools to cultivate lifestyle habits that nurture a fully expressed life.

Writing plays an integral role in how the creative process brings my ideas and intentions to life. I write to capture my interests and ideas and to brainstorm. I write to manipulate my findings and to shape them into conclusions, offerings, and solutions. Think about the habits and practices that support you in evaluating your ideas. Maybe you are a visual person, and you evaluate through drawing or creating charts. You might test your ideas by creating systems and collecting feedback to implement back into your process. You will notice that preparation and verification are externally oriented, and incubation and illumination are internally oriented. This reminds us that we need habits in our lives that nurture our inner worlds as well as how we interact with our outer worlds. It's all connected.

The Courage to Change

My self-care journey started with a promise. I went from not knowing where to start, and not trusting myself, to writing books and leading others in this work. If my limiting beliefs had continued to narrate my story, I would not have been able to realize these manifestations in my life or have an impact on the lives of others. Many of us don't know where to start when it comes to self-care or how to structure our lives to enhance our creative energy and power. The creative process provides a template we can use to ask ourselves what we need in each category of our lives so we can incorporate new behaviors and build new pathways.

This is all so different from the reactive way I used to live, measuring my worth and happiness according to external goals, expectations, and standards. While I am still subject to rules, deadlines, and various types of structure that living in an organized society requires, what's changed is that I no longer accept that I have to respond to these things in a prescribed way.

Instead, I look inside and ask myself: *How do I want to educate myself and my children? How do I want to make a living? How do I want to manage my health?* These are creative decisions that should be driven by our unique needs and aligned with who we authentically are. These decisions absolutely require courage because we are shifting our whole way of being and responding to life—we are drawing in instead of chasing. It doesn't matter what your background, religious beliefs, career path, or roles and responsibilities are; the creative process is a framework that helps you build a fulfilling life that centers your wellness and wholeness. Understanding that your life is part of a universal creative process allows you to do your work in the world with less stress, frustration, and angst. Creative energy doesn't have to be feast or famine. By cultivating habits that support the creative process, you are becoming a more welcoming vessel for ideas and insights to flow through.

I'll tell you like I tell the creatives I work with: Self-care allows the fullest expression of who you are to be released. You were born to be a creator. Your life is your art. When you find yourself drained of creative energy, instead of asking yourself, *What's wrong with me?* start asking yourself, *What do I need?* and know that you *deserve* for your needs to be met. You deserve to take care of yourself. You deserve to set boundaries that protect your mental and physical health. You deserve to make creative choices that invigorate your life. Where you may have been derailed in the past by seasons (or even a lifetime) of overwhelm, disillusionment, or lack of direction, you can turn to the creative process to see which step and corresponding behaviors to activate to give your mind, body, and soul what they need to best support you.

There is no one-size-fits-all when it comes to self-care. Right now you might feel so far removed from this approach to life, and you might be thinking of all the reasons this won't work for you. Remember the goal is not to do a sudden overhaul of everything. We center self-care through gentle shifts and little experiments. Try to implement one change at a time and see how it goes. Observe the differences in how you feel. Take note of the obstacles and distractions so you can experiment with ways to work around them. Maybe your first step is to start taking intentional pauses throughout your day to take deep belly breaths and reset your mind. In those pauses, you are gradually taking back your power.

Before and After

Before I got on this self-care journey, I was constantly sabotaged by the shadow of scarcity. Time, money, energy, ideas, resources—I never had enough. Before, my ideas were watered down, cut short, if not completely abandoned due to self-doubt. If I had an idea that I didn't know how to execute, I would hastily talk myself out of it and try to keep thinking, thinking, thinking of a shortcut. I had no patience, and if I didn't know how to organize my thoughts quickly enough, I would abandon ideas that could have bloomed into blessings. I was emotionally driven and easily overwhelmed because I was disconnected from my center and didn't trust my inner guidance. I took on responsibilities and commitments that were not aligned and then was drained by the effort to follow through, leaving me with less energy for what I truly cared about. I struggled with physical aches and pains, and I was distracted by the chaos in the neglected parts of my life. But with this framework, I was able to find rhythms and synchronize my habits so all the areas of my life are getting love and mindful attention.

When you take care of yourself, you make better decisions. You feel more in harmony with life. You start taking action from a place of worthiness instead of scarcity and finding yourself in relationships and environments where your needs as well as your gifts are valued. You begin to understand how you add a one-of-a-kind energy to every space where you show up authentically.

With healthy rhythms built into our days, we can cope with stressful situations in more productive and beneficial ways. Instead of being reactive with defense mechanisms, we can be proactive with self-care solutions that make us resilient and capable of handling what comes our way.

Reflection: Responsible Choice

Try to realize, and truly realize, that what stands between you and a different life are matters of responsible choice.

—Gary Zukav

My self-care journey has shown me that the strength we need to reclaim our stories and authentically serve our families and communities—the strength I thought would come from suppressing my needs—actually comes from the power of self-care. The impact of all the reflection and mindset shifting we have done in this book will be muted if we don't make responsible choices that align us with the truths and callings we've discovered.

Change requires courage. Sometimes life has to bring us to a scary crossroads before we find the courage to make changes that will shake up our lives. Courage requires change. We need creative courage to break old patterns and begin new chapters. We can't romanticize courage, thinking we'll wake up one day with all the right moves and the resolve to end patterns that have been grooved into our brains our whole lives. To cultivate courage, we have to question our fears, latch on to our values, and hold on for dear life. We have to shift our priorities and center self-care. We start small and practice daily. We tolerate the discomfort. We develop a willingness to deviate from the beaten path so we can figure out what works for us.

What new chapter in your life have you been putting off? Which habits need to change? Which truths need to be expressed? What kind of help do you need? What is the first step? Think about it creatively. Ask yourself how you want to live, how you want to inspire and influence others, and what you want to spend your time doing. Ask yourself which truths and stories you need to express and look inside for the courage to begin.

The most courageous thing we can do is acknowledge that we need and deserve daily replenishment and generously act on this awareness. In this chapter, I shared how I used the four-step creative process to cultivate a lifestyle that centers self-care and fuels my creative energy so I can build a life and career that nourish me. In the exercise below, you will reflect on the habits, activities, and practices that support each step of the creative process so you have actionable ways to bring your reclaimed story to life.

Step One: Preparation

The creative process starts with an idea that you want to acquire knowledge about and expand on to start a project or simply to improve your quality of life. Think of your everyday life as a treasure trove of inspiration and carve out time and space for activities, people, and environments that feed your interests and curiosities.

- Make a list of the habits, activities, and practices that support you in gathering information and ideas that stimulate you in a positive way (*e.g., listening to podcasts, going to the library, engaging in conversations*).
- What do you like about these habits? How do they make you feel? Which parts of you do they stimulate? How do these activities benefit the various parts of your life—physical, mental, creative, professional, social, and spiritual?
- What obstacles and distractions get in the way? What beliefs and boundaries need to change for you to move through them?

Step Two: Incubation

This is the part of the process where we disconnect from focused thinking for a while. When our conscious minds are offline, our DMN gets to work. Our only job is to rest our minds and be present with other valuable aspects of our lives. We often underestimate this necessity and try to power through it.

- Make a list of the habits, activities, and practices that allow you to rest your mind while your ideas simmer (*e.g., exercising, spending quality time with family, engaging in a hobby*).
- What do you like about these habits? How do they make you feel? Which parts of you do they nurture? How do they benefit the various parts of your life—physical, mental, creative, professional, social, and spiritual?
- Which obstacles and distractions get in the way? Which beliefs and boundaries need to change for you to move through them?

Step Three: Illumination

Often, the greatest personal satisfaction occurs in this step, the aha moment. There is a flash of insight or clarity, often while doing something else. It's not always loud or big or clear; it may be a small internal voice that offers a clue, next step, breakthrough, or connection.

- Make a list of habits and practices that invite sudden insights and strengthen your relationship with your intuition (*e.g., prayer and meditation, traveling to new places, therapy*).
- What do you like about these habits? How do they make you feel? Which parts of you do they awaken? How do they benefit the various parts of your life—physical, mental, creative, professional, social, and spiritual?
- Which obstacles and distractions get in the way? Which beliefs and boundaries need to change for you to move through them?

Step Four: Verification

We bring the idea to life and translate it into a usable form in the shape of plans, projects, systems, and life decisions. Using creativity and logic, we bring together all the inputs gathered and formulate an outcome. This does not occur by accident or mood; it requires intention, purpose, and commitment.

- Make a list of the habits and practices that allow you to shape your ideas from raw materials to finished outcomes (*e.g., engaging in creative projects, learning new skills and systems, testing ideas, and solutions*).
- What do you like about these habits? How do they make you feel? Which parts of you do they express? How do they benefit the various parts of your life—physical, mental, creative, professional, social, and spiritual?

- Which obstacles and distractions get in the way? Which beliefs and boundaries need to change for you to move through them?

With the expanded capacity that self-care gave me, I began to wonder what new visions were possible. Which relationships could I restore? Which dreams could become reality?

Chapter Ten

Love and Fear

As I write this, my daughter is learning how to drive. When Rayna is behind the wheel, you can find me in the passenger's seat, holding on to the door handle, pressing my foot down on an invisible brake pedal. I try to relax and enjoy this rite of passage, but I see threats everywhere. I'm fighting the urge to grab the wheel when it looks like she's turning too wide or is about to hit a curb. I'm jumping and calling out, being more of a distraction than a calming presence. I want to let her figure things out, but I don't want her or anyone else to get hurt on my watch.

I went through this process six years ago with my son, Nate, and now he is not only driving but also living on his own, working, paying bills, and making his way in the world. I had to face my fears so he could practice and build the confidence to take his first steps as a young adult. So much of parenting is watching your kids take their first steps, knowing they will inevitably fall but that you will be there to help them get up.

Growing up, I was taught that the only way to move through the world and its inherent risk is to surrender—lean not to your own understanding—and have faith in God. That message clashed with my nervous nature, creating a tug-of-war between fear and faith, a theme in my life. My heart was full of belief, my mind full of doubt.

I was a worried child who often pictured herself rescuing her family from accidents and intruders. I'd lay in bed planning ways for us to escape the house in case of fire. In our red

Cadillac de Ville, I'd sit in the front seat between my mom and dad (which was normal in the '80s) and imagine myself grabbing the wheel to save us from colliding with a drunk driver. At my grandma's house, I plopped at her feet while she braided my hair, and we watched the news. I saw tragedies happening to people all the time—young, old, poor, rich. No one was safe.

I don't think I've ever gotten over that truth about life: bad things happen to good people. I wanted to know what it was all for, what it all means. *Why aren't we all afraid?*

At my request, I got baptized when I was around ten or eleven years old. I loved Jesus and was scared of going to hell, so it was a no-brainer. I bugged my mom about it until she finally agreed on one condition. She said if I was old enough to make this decision, then I should be able to walk down the aisle by myself during the altar call. I was on the youth usher board and was fine with walking up and down the aisles, but this was different. This time I was making a statement in front of everyone. I might be crying or clumsy with emotion as I took those steps, but I was willing. My sense of purpose transcended my fear.

The following Sunday morning when the sermon was over, the pastor called out, "The doors of the church are open! Won't you come?" When I didn't get up right away, Mom squeezed my hand. I looked up to see the assurance in her eyes before floating down the aisle, then one of the deacons led me to the front pew.

That was the first step. Before the baptism could take place, I had to attend four foundational classes over four weeks to ensure I knew exactly what I was signing up for. By giving my life to Christ, I was accepting Him as my personal savior and acknowledging that He died on the cross so I could have eternal life. In my young mind, the baptism would change me. It would wash away my fear and make me holy. I wouldn't sin anymore, and if I did, because of Jesus's sacrifice, I would be forgiven. His blood would cover and protect me.

I had questions about this: *Would I be protected from danger more than an unbaptized child? Why aren't the love and kindness in someone's heart more important than whether or not they've been baptized or what religion they were born into? Is God somewhere up there in the sky, or is God inside of me?* But I was told not to question, only to believe and have faith. One day, it would all make sense.

A few seconds. That's how long I was told I would be underwater. The night before the baptism, I lay in bed testing how long I could hold my breath. *What's a few seconds—five, ten, fifteen? What if I panic?* I prayed for the Holy Spirit to calm me, I prayed for Jesus to hold my hand, and I prayed that God wouldn't let me drown in the baptismal tub.

In the morning, the choir sang "Take Me to the Water" as we lined up to be saved. Wearing an oversized all-white gown, I hoped no one could see me shaking underneath. I inhaled with all my might before the pastor and his assistant plunged me into the warm water, a trust fall into salvation. I was only under for a second or two, but I came up gasping for air, dizzy with panic. It was a sacred experience, but I was disappointed to feel the same on the way up as I did on the way down—afraid.

This was the beginning of my faith journey, which would turn out to be an ongoing tension between love and fear. I wanted the baptism to bring me closer to God, but it was also transactional. I do this; now God does that. I wanted to feel safe. Ultimately, it didn't make my fear or my questions go away, and it didn't give me the certainty I craved. It may have even confused me more.

A few years later when I was in my teens, my relationship with God became further complicated by religion. My mother started to study and practice different religions, mainly Judaism. Throughout my adolescence, we would celebrate the Christian holidays like Easter and Christmas and the Jewish high holidays like Rosh Hashanah and Yom Kippur. We lit candles and kept the Sabbath from sundown Friday to sundown Saturday, and we went to church to stomp our feet and clap our hands on Sunday morning. I ate kosher when I was with my mother, and I ate secular when I was away from her with my friends.

This medley of religion changed the way I perceived faith as I took my first steps into adulthood. In seeking God, I was seeking unconditional love, hope, and a source of comfort, something changeless to focus on to counteract the volatility of life. My twenties led me away from Christianity to a more pluralistic view of faith. The higher power that I felt in the vibrations of the choir, in a leap across a recital stage, in an act of kindness was no longer contained by a specific religion. It is the Love that runs through all of it. It is impossible to touch and impossible to live without. It is the source of all creative energy. Call it God, Allah, Source, Spirit. The most universal of them all to me is Love. Love lets us take whatever path we choose to enlightenment. Love does not insist on its own way. Love casts out fear. The commitment to choose love over fear is the salvation I'd been seeking all along.

I repeat these words to myself when I'm sitting in the passenger seat next to my daughter: *Love over fear.* I relax my grip on the door handle and slow my breathing. I reason with myself, *Which one is in control here*? This will be a core memory one day. I don't want fear to dominate another precious occasion. I want to be present, and I want this to be a positive experience for her. I could focus on everything that could go wrong, or I could say a prayer and let go. In these moments, I breathe in love and breathe out fear. I breathe in faith and breathe out surrender.

Routinely, fear tells me that I will fail. Fear tells me that I will hurt someone or be hurt. It tells me that I will make a terrible mistake. Love tells me that any of these things can happen, and I will still be okay. Love tells me it is bigger than any moment I might face. I need this assurance, always have. So I start each day with surrender to let go of my fears and embrace the fullness of life.

What does faith mean to you? What higher power or inner resource do you turn to for guidance and comfort? How did that belief system develop? How does it support you? If you don't have a belief system, what sustains you when you lose hope?

Full Circle

Choosing love is a risk because it makes us vulnerable, while choosing fear often feels more protective. Fear disguises itself as practicality and says, *If I don't try, I can't fail. If I do things the way they've always been done, I'll be safe. If I'm not emotionally available, I can't be hurt.*

We think our comfort zones will secure and satisfy us, but they only dim our light and numb our power. Without the risk that comes with choosing love, our lives are made smaller; our dreams fade into the distance.

Choosing love is hard when you have unhealed wounds, especially when you're unaware of them. In my twenties and thirties, of all the challenges I faced, motherhood resurfaced the most vulnerable parts of me. Sometimes when I see my daughter's temper, or my son's self-doubt, or my other daughter's anxiety, I blame myself for any emotional wounds I may have passed on to them. I know, I know. There is no such thing as a perfect parent, and difficulty is not optional in this life. But I don't want them to remember their childhoods as something they have to recover from. Fear tells me I could have done better. It makes me wish I knew then what I know now. But I realize that my mistakes clarified my values, and my kids are a huge part of what motivated me to heal, a journey I talk about with them often, especially as they get older. Love tells me that everything happened the way it needed to and that they have their own journey, their own part of the tapestry.

Watching Rayna behind the wheel, I remember when I was the newbie in the driver's seat and my mother was the passenger. Somehow she managed to show up for me for the big things even as her mental health was steadily declining. In my teens, she seemed to be one foot in this reality and one foot in hers. Her delusion was obvious, but so was her devotion to me.

She fueled my love for learning. She made sure I knew God. She exposed me to art. She put me in college preparatory programs and environments where high achievement was the norm. She cheered me on through college and graduation, even as she was struggling to keep a roof over her head. Even as she navigated a reality where everyone she loved was also a threat. And later, she was a doting grandma, complete with cartoon voices and silly dances. I remember how the kids brought her eyes to life and turned her fear into love. She had a tug-of-war going on inside of her too.

I wish I knew the secrets that shaped her story. How she became who she became. I am left with bits and pieces of memory and lore from family members and photos: snapshots of her as a young girl with cat-eye glasses in the '50s; a young, hot mom in a bikini lounging at the pool with my brother in the '60s; a newlywed staring up at my dad at Niagara Falls in the '70s. Eyes full of promise. I miss the mother she was and the woman I never knew.

I did have a childhood that I had to recover from, but that didn't make it any less beautiful. Fear tells me that if I'd had a "normal" childhood, I would not have struggled so much. Love tells me to count it all joy.

My time with my parents was cut short due to illness, avoidance, and silence. For my mother and me, avoidance led to estrangement, and when I'm in a low place, that fact feels like failure. Fear says I failed my mom. Fear says I failed myself. But love says that story doesn't leave room for hope. Love says that she and I are still writing our story.

Reclaiming the Narrative

Reclaiming your story is a vulnerable act. It requires faith, a deep trust in love, and an awareness of what you hold sacred. Faith to believe that you can heal and your story can change. Faith to believe there is something universal that holds and fuels and fills you. Faith to release old beliefs and embrace new ideas that can shepherd you into your next chapter. Faith to break silences and cycles, to let the truth set you free. It requires faith to believe that your creative vision can be brought to life through daily choices. It is not a faith that guarantees a specific result; it is a faith that promises meaning.

As a child, the stories I told myself were fueled by my fixation on the worst that could happen. Reclaiming my story was about recognizing the impact of fear on my life and answering the call to love that I heard way back then. The call that showed up as sacred missions—to get baptized and give my life to Christ, to deviate from the religion that raised me, to pursue creativity as a spiritual practice, to end the cycle of silence and avoidance, with the faith that facing my fears would be worthwhile.

The helplessness of watching my mom worsen over the years and not doing anything about it followed me into adulthood. I carried unspoken shame and guilt about the dissolution of my family, and I didn't trust myself. But writing changed all of that. Writing broke the silence and revealed a new storyline. Through writing, I found my voice and a path to meaning.

I discovered I could face anything if I could integrate it into my existence, learn from it, and make it part of my wholeness and sense of purpose. What could revising your story reveal to you?

There is profound healing in self-discovery and storytelling. Past experiences don't have to be reasons for regret or stagnation; they can be starting points for new ways of being. Your past is a treasure trove of untapped wisdom, and in *Story Work*, we have treasure hunted together.

We have gone back to our roots and origins to face our inner questions, the puzzles that life keeps presenting to us in a myriad of ways. We have considered what else could be true when it comes to the limiting beliefs and assumptions we've made about life and our roles in it. We have examined the facts, our feelings, and our hindsight view to find healing narratives that shine a light on the lessons we've learned, even from the most difficult experiences. We've plugged our stories into creative narrative arcs to find storylines for our lives, which highlight our transformations and turning points.

We reflected on truths and lies to gain insights about our authentic values, not the ones we inherited but the ones we are innately moved by, so they can guide us as we reframe meaning and reclaim our stories. With our values recentered, we felt lighter until we discovered more layers of fear and pretense. We learned how to offer ourselves grace as we continue to work through patterns that we don't want and blind spots we can't see. We celebrated that our differences are not reasons to hide or feel shame, and when we recognize our differences as strengths, they become superpowers that we can use to enrich our lives and the lives of others. We talked about keeping our arms open for the fullness of the story, the beginnings as well as the endings.

Our voices and visions are brought to life through the power of our words and habits. We have reconnected with our truths, values, gifts, and strengths, and now it's time to bring them to life with our daily choices. We got curious about our thoughts, how our minds can work in service of our hearts instead of our fears, and how we design our lives to be in service of the stories we want to tell. We asked ourselves: *Who do I want to be? To be that kind of person, what do I need to be doing? How do I want to feel? What kinds of habits and practices make me feel that way?* You are walking away with the understanding that *the being* and *the doing* work together to create the life you want.

The best way to reclaim your story and point your life in a direction that inspires and fulfills you each day is to surrender to what lights you up and steer your ship in the direction of it. Choosing love over fear gives you creative control to make the difference you are here to make. We need to embody the changes we want to see in ourselves and the world. So the questions become: What is your creative vision for your life? What is the reclaimed story you want your life to tell?

Surrender to Your Creative Callings

The discovery that pain has a purpose sparked my creativity and opened doors. The process is more profound than I ever imagined. We've all been wounded, bruised, broken, and afraid, and we carry around the scabs and scars from those experiences. But the wound doesn't have to be the end; it can be a beginning. The pain can illuminate what we value and become a calling to focus on that value. We may feel regret, shame, guilt, and distrust from the wounds we've received and the ones we've caused, but without them, we wouldn't have the wisdom and clarity we have today. Wherever there is hurt, there is room to heal, and in the discomfort of healing, there is an experience of meaning. Our wounds gave us fear, but they can also teach us love.

There is a beautiful connection between our pain and our gifts, and it all comes together to create the one-of-a-kind medicine that each of us has to offer. Susan Cain describes it in

Bittersweet: How Sorrow and Longing Make Us Whole: "What is the ache you can't get rid of—and could you make it your creative offering?"

Our lives are fueled by our callings. If you are asking, "But what is my calling?" it is not necessarily one specific offering but a call to be obedient to a certain sacred guidance from within—a call to heal. A calling is a source of hope, something you aspire to align with and believe in. It can show up in different ways in different seasons.

Have you ever had a calling to read a certain book, talk to a certain person, or visit a certain place? Have you ever felt drawn to write a poem or to pick up a guitar or a paintbrush? Maybe you have felt a calling to join a certain group or take a class. Do you daydream about teaching, traveling, leaving, starting over, aiming higher, expanding? What's more important than the specifics of the calling is who you become and how your story evolves as you surrender to that calling. It's the faith you develop, the relationship you build with your inner knowing that transcends the fear of the unknown.

Your calling will light you up, and what lights you up also lights up the world. As you project your healing outward, you heal others.

Let's say your calling right now as you come to the end of this book is to take a first step toward reclaiming your story. Fear might tell you it's too late. Why dig up all these layers? Why make yourself vulnerable? Fear might say it won't make a difference in your life or anyone else's. Love says listening to your callings could change your life. Love says your story could inspire someone else to keep going, to see something in their lives differently. Love says your story could be the thing that gives someone hope.

Somewhere just beyond your comfort zone, there are answers to the questions your heart has been asking. The distance is less than you think, and the possibilities are more than you know.

What have you been through that gives you a creative offering? How could your story help others? If you believed that storytelling could empower you and make a difference in the world, how would you tell your story? What would it look like for you to choose love over fear? What's at stake?

Collective Responsibility

Here in the United States, we don't know what this country will look like over the next four years. It's 2024, and the new president-elect is a man who thrives on stoking fear, division, and hate in the country he says he wants to make great again. Those of us who value unity, diversity, and democracy can shake our heads and lick our wounds, but at some point, we have to move forward. We will survive this. Even those of us who choose to leave the country must reckon with the unhealed trauma in our bodies that we carry with us.

American society carries centuries of unhealed trauma that has been passed down through generations. In *My Grandmother's Hands: Racialized Trauma and the Mending of Our Bodies and Hearts*, Resmaa Menakem describes trauma through the lens of clean pain and dirty pain: "Healing trauma involves recognizing, accepting, and moving through pain—clean pain. It often means facing what you don't want to face—what you have been reflexively avoiding or fleeing. By walking into that pain, experiencing it fully, and moving through it, you metabolize it and put an end to it." He goes on to say, "The alternative paths of avoidance, blame, and denial are paved with dirty pain. When people respond from their most wounded parts and choose dirty pain, they only create more of it, both for themselves and for other people."

In America, we've been told stories that have prevented healing and restoration. We've kept silences that have perpetuated more trauma and brokenness within and across intersectional groups. So, you see, reclaiming our stories must start with each person, and it doesn't end there. The healing that begins in our bodies, where our stories live, radiates outward to reshape history, the here and now, and future generations.

Wherever you are in the world, as you are reclaiming your story, you are also reckoning with the larger story of the families, tribes, communities, towns, and countries that you and your ancestors have called home, whether by choice or by force. Our histories are part of our everyday lives. Menakem says that when we heal, we create more room for growth in our nervous systems. We need to know where we come from and what we've been through to better understand what we need so we can pass on the wisdom of clean pain and healing practices to future generations. We must ask ourselves—on a personal and collective level—if we are facing our challenges with honesty and vulnerability or if we are avoiding and denying inconvenient truths. Clean pain is about choosing love over fear.

Fear says if I can't solve the entire problem, then I can't do anything. Love says I can use my callings to contribute to healing and change. Do you feel a responsibility to heal that is bigger than yourself?

Reflecting on this question, I thought of my Baptist upbringing and how I was raised to praise God without ceasing and to count my blessings. Many years and spiritual evolutions later, I approach my creative practice as a form of worship, a duty that steadies me in gratitude. I do feel a sense of duty to honor my divine instincts and give birth to the work that wants to come through me. As a Black woman and mother, I feel a responsibility to pass on empowering narratives and healthy practices to my descendants and future generations. As a writer, I feel a responsibility to assert my truths, even at the risk, in the spirit of Audre Lorde, of having them bruised or misunderstood. As a coach, I feel a responsibility to empower other humans to discover, reclaim, and share their stories. I have a duty to humanity to be a creator. I have a responsibility to offer hope and cause less harm in the world.

The callings you have are yours for a reason. They are lights guiding you toward your next becoming, to truer versions of yourself, which leads to a more loving, unified version of the world. We're not all meant to serve in the same way, and your special medicine is needed. What can you do today that your future self will thank you for? What can you do today that future generations will thank you for?

Reclaiming Love

How do we maintain our conviction and take care of ourselves as we move forward, facing the challenges that healing presents, inside and out? How do we face the tension between love and fear?

We start with self-honesty. We practice radical self-care because we know that healthy habits replenish our minds, bodies, and souls. We balance self-nurturance with service to others and make collective healing part of our creative vision. We find unique ways to share our resources, ideas, joys, and passions with the world. We don't get lost in roles, expectations, and labels. We learn how to protect our energy and harness our power. By serving in ways that honor our true nature, we honor our ancestors and plant seeds for our descendants. We give each other hope.

When in doubt, we have faith in what we hope for but can't yet see. We lean into each other. We surround ourselves with people we can learn and grow with, who hold space for our vision, who hold us accountable and cheer for us. We get out of our heads and into our bodies to sit with the discomfort of transformation. We have faith that what we don't know, we can learn. We trust the process. We surrender to the unknown by choosing love over fear.

In the past, fear may have told you that you're a victim and your role is set in stone. But love says you are a hero, a survivor, a storyteller with a message. As you reclaim your story, you are reclaiming love. What if choosing love over fear is the salvation we need to unite us all?

Reflection: Surrender to Your Calling

> *Helped are those who create anything at all, for they shall relive the thrill of their own conception, and realize a partnership in the creation of the Universe that keeps them responsible and cheerful.*
>
> —Alice Walker

Reclaiming your story is an act of faith. After reading this book, I hope you will continue to use writing as a tool to further your story work. Write with the faith that when you surrender your truths to the page, you will heal wounds and unlock mysteries; you will gain access to something bigger than yourself expressing itself through you.

Reclaiming your story is a calling. My hope is that you are thinking about what's next for you with a renewed sense of possibility. The path to change starts wherever you are. My dream is that you will read this book and recommit yourself to your creative callings. It's never too soon and it's never too late to center your values and embrace your creative identity.

Reclaiming your story is bigger than you. I hope you have a renewed curiosity about the broader stories you are part of—your family, your community, and the world. Remember that your contribution to the story matters.

Story Work is a reminder to turn inward. Your creative urges come from stories inside that need to emerge. By giving yourself permission to reclaim the stories that have limited you in the past, you are inviting the world to open up to you in new ways.

For our last exercise, reflect on the following prompts:

- What is your creative vision for your life? If you followed the joy and meaning in your life, where would they lead you?
- What does fear say about your creative vision? What are the doubts and distractions that come to mind?
- What does love say about it? What do you need to believe in order to follow your heart?

Notes

Introduction

9 ***As Toni Morrison said:*** "Commencement Speeches: Wellesley College Commencement Address," C-Span, May 28, 2004, https://www.c-span.org/program/commencement-speeches/wellesley-college-commencement-address/129052.

Chapter 1: Months Turned into Years

24 ***In her first published book:*** Anaïs Nin, *D. H. Lawrence: An Unprofessional Study* (Swallow Press, 1964).

24 ***She goes on to say:*** Maria Popova, "How to Be Un-Dead: Anaïs Nin and D.H. Lawrence on the Key to Living Fully," The Marginalian, accessed February 3, 2025, https://www.themarginalian.org/2022/11/02/anais-nin-d-h-lawrence/.

Chapter 2: Smile and Wave

35 ***"If illusions are valued":*** bell hooks, *Sisters of the Yam: Black Women and Self-Recovery*, 2nd ed. (Routledge, 2014), 24.

37 ***"An insight is an unexpected":*** Scott Barry Kaufman and Carolyn Gregoire, *Wired to Create: Unraveling the Mysteries of the Creative Mind* (Perigee, 2017), 69.

38 ***"There is a crack":*** Leonard Cohen, "Anthem," November 24, 1992, https://genius.com/Leonard-cohen-anthem-lyrics.

39 ***"Love makes pain":*** G. G. Renee Hill, *The Beautiful Disruption: A Soul Story* (CreateSpace Independent Publishing Platform, 2014), 137.

Chapter 3: Fatal Flaw

48 ***"relief":*** Yrsa Daley-Ward, *Bone* (Penguin, 2017), 21.
50 ***"The 'Strong Black Woman'":*** Scholars Strategy Network, "How the Expectation of Strength Harms Black Girls and Women," August 15, 2019, https://scholars.org/contribution/how-expectation-strength-harms-black-girls-and.
50 ***In her study:*** Scholars Strategy Network, "How the Expectation of Strength Harms Black Girls and Women."
52 ***Complex trauma is a psychological condition:*** Hilary I. Lebow, "What Is Complex Trauma and How Does It Develop?," PsychCentral, July 2, 2021, https://psychcentral.com/ptsd/complex-trauma-a-step-by-step-description-of-how-it-develops.
56 ***In her memoir What My Bones Know:*** Stephanie Foo, *What My Bones Know* (Ballantine Books, 2023).
56 ***"We are all products":*** Rachel Zimmerman, "How Does Trauma Spill from One Generation to the Next?," *Washington Post*, June 12, 2023, https://www.washingtonpost.com/wellness/2023/06/12/generational-trauma-passed-healing/.
58 ***In his book, The Seven Basic Plots:*** Christopher Booker, *The Seven Basic Plots: Why We Tell Stories* (Bloomsbury Continuum, 2019).

Chapter 4: Masks We Wear

81 ***"Our deeper understanding":*** Gary Zukav, *The Seat of the Soul*, Anniversary ed. (Simon & Schuster, 2014), 10.
82 ***"Vulnerability minus boundaries is not vulnerability":*** Jessica Stillman, "How Much Vulnerability at Work Is Too Much? Brené Brown Just Explained in 6 Words," Inc.com, March 5, 2021, https://www.inc.com/jessica-stillman/brene-brown-leadership-vulnerability/authenticity.html.
82 ***"Are you sharing your":*** Stillman, "How Much Vulnerability."
84 ***when you plant compatible plants near each other:*** University of Portsmouth, "Plants Might Be Helping Each Other More than Thought," ScienceDaily, November 2019, https://www.sciencedaily.com/releases/2019/11/191113095246.htm.

Chapter 5: The Unreliable Narrator

101 ***lying requires a huge amount of brain power:*** Yan Li, Zhiwei Liu, and Xiping Liu, "More Lies Lead to More Memory Impairments in Daily Life," *Frontiers in Psychology* 13 (2022): 822788, https://doi.org/10.3389/fpsyg.2022.822788.

103 ***"Mindfulness not only":*** Bessel A. Van der Kolk, *The Body Keeps the Score: Brain, Mind, and Body in the Healing of Trauma* (Penguin, 2015).

105 ***"If you live in the dark":*** Mary Karr, *Lit*, repr. ed. (Harper Perennial, 2010).

Chapter 6: Strengths and Superpowers

112 ***"She's sensitive, too":*** Junot Diaz, *This Is How You Lose Her*, repr. ed. (Riverhead Books, 2013).

115 ***"The universe buries strange":*** Elizabeth Gilbert, *Big Magic: Creative Living Beyond Fear*, repr. ed. (Riverhead Books, 2016), 8.

118 ***"The Victim is the character":*** Donald Miller, *Hero on a Mission: A Path to a Meaningful Life* (HarperCollins Leadership, 2022), xiii.

118 ***"All we need to know":*** Miller, *Hero on a Mission*, 5.

Chapter 7: Nothing Is Ever Lost

128 ***"a tendency to states":*** Susan Cain, *Bittersweet: How Sorrow and Longing Make Us Whole* (Crown, 2023).

134 ***"We don't know":*** Chimamanda Ngozi Adichie, *Notes on Grief* (Knopf, 2021).

136 ***Grief can manifest physically in body aches:*** Nisha Kikunga, "The Physical Pain of Grief: 4 Things You Can Do to Help," Vori Health, accessed January 1, 2025, https://www.vorihealth.com/resource/the-physical-pain-of-grief-4-things-you-can-do-to-help.

141 ***"Letting there be room":*** Pema Chödrön, *When Things Fall Apart: Heart Advice for Difficult Times*, Anniversary ed. (Shambhala, 2016).

145 ***"Nostalgia is uniquely positioned among emotions":*** Wijnand A. P. van Tilburg, "Locating Nostalgia Among the Emotions: A Bridge from Loss to Love," *Current Opinion in Psychology* 49 (February 2023): 101543, https://www.sciencedirect.com/science/article/pii/s2352250x22002640.

146 ***"Every new beginning":*** Semisonic, "Closing Time," March 10, 1998, https://genius.com/Semisonic-closing-time-lyrics.

Chapter 8: The Power of Words

154 ***The subject of reclaiming our thoughts:*** Kelly Bilodeau, "Managing Intrusive Thoughts," Harvard Health Publishing, March 26, 2024, https://www.health.harvard.edu/mind-and-mood/managing-intrusive-thoughts.

156 ***Cognitive distortions are biased thoughts:*** D. M. Pollock, "What Are Cognitive Distortions?," Medical News Today, November 29, 2023, https://www.medicalnewstoday.com/articles/cognitive-distortions.

156 ***the brain creates mental filters as shortcuts:*** "Cognitive Distortion," APA Dictionary of Psychology, April 19, 2018, https://dictionary.apa.org/cognitive-distortion.

158 ***In Loving What Is:*** Byron Katie, *Loving What Is: Four Questions That Can Change Your Life*, rev. ed. (Harmony, 2021).

159 ***Neuroplasticity is the brain's ability:*** Matt Puderbaugh and Prabhu D. Emmady, "Neuroplasticity," National Library of Medicine, May 1, 2023, https://www.ncbi.nlm.nih.gov/books/nbk557811.

159 ***Neural pathways are the connections:*** "Neural Pathways: How Your Mind Stores the Info and Thoughts That Affect Your Behaviour," accessed January 1, 2025, https://lifexchangesolutions.com/neural-pathways/.

160 ***This is because when:*** Rick Hanson, *Hardwiring Happiness: The New Brain Science of Contentment, Calm, and Confidence* (Harmony, 2013).

160 ***Toxic positivity is when we misuse optimism:*** Sara-Mai Conway, "Spiritual Bypassing and How to Avoid It," Mindworks, accessed January 1, 2025, htttps://mindworks.org/blog/spiritual-bypassing-how-to-avoid.

Chapter 9: Life as a Creative Process

178 ***these health issues are higher in Black people:*** Arline T. Geronimus et al., "'Weathering' and Age Patterns of Allostatic Load Scores Among Blacks and Whites in the United States," *American Journal of Public Health* 96, no. 5 (May 2006): 826–833, https://pmc.ncbi.nlm.nih.gov/articles/pmc1470581.

181 ***He said that I have dense breasts:*** Mayo Clinic Staff, "Dense Breast Tissue: What It Means to Have Dense Breasts," Mayo Clinic, March 9, 2024, https://mayoclinic.org/tests-procedures/mammogram/in-depth,dense-breast-tissue/art-20123968.

182 ***According to the EMDR Institute:*** EMDR Institute, "EMDR: A Revolutionary Approach to Healing," accessed February 5, 2025, https://www.emdr.com/what-is-emdr-therapy-layperson/.

182 ***Walking also supports:*** Kaufman and Gregoire, *Wired to Create*, 40–41.

184 ***"Courage is the most":*** Anne Ju, "Courage Is the Most Important Virtue, Says Writer and Civil Rights Activist Maya Angelou at Convocation," *Cornell Chronicle*, May 24, 2008, https://news.cornell.edu/stories/2008/05/courage-most-important-virtue-maya-angelou-tells-seniors.

188 ***"Good habits create":*** Rick Rubin, *The Creative Act: A Way of Being* (Penguin, 2023).

190 ***The first step is preparation:*** Carolyn Gregoire, "Understanding the Four Stages of the Creative Process," WeWork, October 18, 2019, https://wework.com/ideas/professional-development/creativity-culture/understandin-the-four-stages-of-the-creative-process.

193 ***The DMN is a system of connected brain areas:*** Thomas Z. Ramsøy, "Creativity, Mind-Wandering, and the Default Mode Network of the Brain," accessed January 1, 2025, https://thomasramsoy.com/index.php/2024/08/26/creativity-mind-wandering-and-the-default-mode-network-of-the-brain/.

Chapter 10: Love and Fear

216 ***"What is the ache":*** Cain, *Bittersweet*, 6.

217 ***"Healing trauma involves":*** Resmaa Menakem, *My Grandmother's Hands: Racialized Trauma and the Mending of Our Bodies and Hearts* (Central Recovery Press, 2017), 165.

217 ***"The alternative paths":*** Menakem, *My Grandmother's Hands*, 166.